The Silence of the Shuttered Window

AAMIR KHAN

BlueRose ONE.com
Stories Matter
NewDelhi • London

BLUEROSE PUBLISHERS

India | U.K.

BlueRose ONE.com
Stories Matter
NewDelhi • London

For permissions requests or inquiries regarding this publication, please contact:

BLUEROSE PUBLISHERS
www.BlueRoseONE.com
info@bluerosepublishers.com
+91 8882 898 898
+4407342408967

ISBN: 978-93-7310-374-7

Cover design: Yash Singhal
Typesetting: Namrata Saini

First Edition: November 2025

Dedication

I dedicate this novel to all the girls who have suffered in quiet violence from any injustice, pain, or oppression. My heart goes out to each one of them, and I sincerely pray that no girl ever has to endure any wrongdoing. May the world become a safer, kinder place where every woman is treated with the respect, dignity, and love she truly deserves.

Acknowledgement

Writing a story and seeing it through to the end is never easy. Many stories remain unfinished or, limited, ending before they even get a chance to breathe. I am truly grateful to God for giving me the strength to write about the plight of a daughter who faced atrocities no one can comprehend without a heartache.

My heartfelt gratitude goes to my mother, father, and brother, whose unwavering support and encouragement have been my guiding light. Their presence has been a constant source of strength, inspiring me throughout this journey.

I am also deeply thankful to the dedicated team at Blue Rose Publishers, whose invaluable assistance and steadfast support has been with me at every step of this process. Their belief in my vision alongside their commitment in providing me with this incredible platform have allowed me to share this poignant tale with the world. Their contribution has been instrumental in bringing this story to life, and I will always be indebted to them.

despite my desperate efforts to contain them. I could scarcely believe that humanity had deteriorated to such a degree, ruthlessly seizing every opportunity to dismantle the very essence of our humanity.

"My mind is constantly occupied with the question of why God creates such people. Perhaps I'm using the wrong word— *'why are such beasts created'*—who have no right to breathe on this earth?"

A daughter is writhing in pain,
A son is tearing apart her honor.

A daughter was pleading with folded hands,
While a son was laughing at her plight.

When God crafted those beasts, it was perhaps beyond His imagination that such mishaps would emerge into the world. These beings, devoid of any semblance of humanity, would walk among us, incapable of feeling or understanding the pain of others.

A tormented daughter cries out to God, her voice trembling with desperation: *"Rescue me from these monsters. What have I done to deserve this? Why am I being punished in this way?"*

Contents

Not a Dream, But the True Essence

For as long as anyone could remember, the Mehra household had been longing for her.

Not a name, not a face—just a soft vision wrapped in pink cotton and jasmine-scented lullabies. A daughter, a little girl whose presence had been dreamt into every corner of the home, even though she had never arrived.

The family's life moved forward, year by year, but always with a tender void at its center. Sons were celebrated, cousins grew older, and weddings were held—but in the hush of the night, someone would always glance at the empty cradle tucked away in the attic, untouched and dusted with hope.

They had tried everything.

From ancient temples nestled in the folds of the Himalayas to the sunlit shores of southern shrines, they traveled with folded hands and hearts full of longing. The family matriarch, her bangles clinking like wind chimes, lit oil lamps in silence, her whispered prayers rising with the scent of sandalwood and marigold.

But faith, for them, was not confined to one path. It flowed like a river, winding through belief and devotion, carrying their prayers wherever hope might listen.

They tied sacred threads at Dargahs, the cool marble under their knees and the rustle of rose petals in the breeze. In the quiet halls of Gurdwaras, they bowed low, their eyes closed tightly, pressing their dreams into the earth with every prayer.

No distance felt too far. No ritual too much. Because somewhere, in some quiet corner of the universe, they believed a soul was waiting to come home. A daughter, born not just of flesh and blood, but of patience, faith, and endless love.

And even though her tiny feet had never touched the floor, her presence was everywhere—in the songs that were never sung, in the anklets that never chimed, and in the hearts that had made space for her long before she existed.

She was hope, wrapped in silence.

And they would wait as long as it took for her to arrive.

Chirag glanced over at Aashvi, concerned etching deep lines across his forehead. Something about her expression unsettled him—pale, uneasy, distant.

"Aashvi, what's wrong?" he asked, stepping closer.

She leaned against the wall for support, her face drawn and her breathing uneven. *"I don't know, Chirag... I'm feeling very strange. My head is spinning, and I've been vomiting since morning."*

A moment of silence passed between them. Then a flicker of hope lit up Chirag's eyes. His voice dropped, almost to a whisper. *"Could it be...?"* He took a deep breath. *"Maybe God has finally answered our prayers. Maybe you're going to be the mother of my daughter."*

Aashvi looked up at him, wide-eyed, the corners of her lips trembling into a smile. Despite the discomfort clouding her body, a wave of warmth spread through her chest. *"If that's true,"* *she said softly,* *"it would be the happiest news of my life."*

Chirag reached for her hand, gently squeezing it. *"We shouldn't wait or assume anything. Let's go see a doctor—he'll be able to tell us for sure."*

Aashvi nodded, the faint glow of hope now mingling with her nerves. Together, they stepped out, hearts pounding with anticipation and a quiet sense of wonder.

The car rolled to a gentle stop in front of a towering white building, its glass doors reflecting the soft morning sun. Above the entrance, in bold blue letters, the sign read: MAX Hospital.

Chirag stepped out first, opening the door for Aashvi with quiet urgency. As she placed a cautious foot on the pavement, her heart pounded—not just from the queasy feeling in her stomach, but from the uncertainty wrapped around the moment. Together, hand in hand, they walked toward the hospital doors, each step echoing with a strange mixture of excitement and fear.

Inside, the sterile scent of antiseptic met them, but neither noticed. Their minds were too full.

This day—this very moment—was something their hearts had whispered about for years. For generations, the family had waited for the delicate laughter of a daughter to dance through their home. A little girl. A princess. Not out of preference, but out of a longing that had grown deeper with time, passed down like a prayer from one heart to the next.

Their faith had become their anchor. Temples, dargahs, gurdwaras—no door had been left unopened. And now, they truly believed that God was ready to bless them. That Aashvi was carrying their long-awaited miracle. Soon, a tiny heartbeat would be echoing inside her—a promise of pink bangles and soft lullabies.

But beneath that faith, a quiet fear simmered.

What if the test said otherwise?

What if this hope, so carefully cradled, shattered in a matter of minutes?

Aashvi clutched Chirag's hand a little tighter, as if trying to hold onto something real—something that could carry them through whatever news awaited beyond the waiting room. He glanced at her, offering a small, reassuring smile, though his own nerves danced just beneath the surface.

They didn't speak as they reached the reception. Words felt too fragile.

In that moment, suspended between prayer and possibility, they waited.

Not just for a test result—but for a dream that had taken years to bloom.

"Doctor, my wife's health has suddenly worsened, and she's feeling dizzy. I think she might be pregnant."

"This is wonderful news, but how can you be sure that she is pregnant? Has your wife taken a pregnancy test?" the doctor said.

Aashvi's voice is heard, *"No, doctor, I haven't done a pregnancy test yet."*

"I am writing a prescription for a pregnancy test. Please have it done, and the result will confirm whether you are going to be parents."

Following the nurse's quiet gesture, Aashvi slowly stepped through the corridor, her heart thudding louder with each passing second. The walls, sterile and white, seemed to close in slightly as she walked ahead—alone now—toward the room where her tests would begin.

She cast one last glance over her shoulder.

Chirag stood by the waiting area, his hands clenched into fists inside his pockets, trying to mask the storm brewing inside him. Their eyes met briefly—just a moment—but it was enough to say everything they couldn't voice aloud.

Aashvi disappeared behind the door.

Chirag let out a slow breath, settling into the hard plastic chair outside, but there was no comfort in sitting still. The seconds ticked by like hours, each one stretching thin under the weight of uncertainty. His leg bounced nervously, his mind torn between hope and fear.

The door creaked open at last, and for a fleeting second, Chirag caught a glimpse of Aashvi.

Just that one look—pale yet composed, eyes searching for his—was enough to send a wave of restlessness through him. His heart skipped, then quickened, as if sensing that everything was about to change. He rose instinctively, unable to stay still, the anticipation tightening in his chest like a knot.

Something in her expression made his breath catch—was it relief, or was it fear?

"Chirag... the results are in—I'm pregnant." Her voice trembled with joy, her eyes shimmering with emotion. *"I'm so overwhelmed with happiness today... I can hardly find the words."*

That moment had changed everything.

From that day on, Chirag became more than just a husband—he became her shadow, her protector, and her constant comfort. Every craving, every mood swing, every ounce of morning sickness—he was there. He would wake before dawn to prepare her ginger tea, keep her warm compress ready during the evenings, and place gentle hands on her back when the weight of it all became too much.

He read parenting books in secret, marked pages about nutrition, and learned how to count baby kicks with a seriousness that made her laugh. He'd even speak to her growing belly at night in a soft, hopeful voice, whispering stories to the little life forming within her.

And through it all, Aashvi bloomed—fragile yet radiant, tired but glowing. Pregnancy had changed her body, yes, but it had deepened her soul. And Chirag admired her more with each passing day.

Now, nine months later, after a journey full of anticipation and gentle care, Aashvi had been admitted to the hospital for her operation. The long wait was nearly over.

But once again, Chirag found himself sitting alone.

The sterile white walls, the faint scent of antiseptic, the ticking clock above the doorway—none of it could pull his thoughts away from her. He sat in the same waiting room where their journey had begun months ago; only now, he wasn't wondering *if* they would become parents—he was wondering when he would hold their child in his arms.

His hands trembled slightly. He missed her—not just her smile or the way she teased him when he fussed too much—but the quiet strength she gave him simply by being nearby.

As the doors to the operating theatre closed behind her, he bowed his head and held on to one prayer, the only one that mattered now—

Let her be safe. Let our daughter arrive in this world wrapped in her mother's strength and my love.

And with that, the next chapter of their story prepared to unfold—
Not just the birth of a child, but the rebirth of two hearts as parents.

The wife who stood by him through every twist and turn,
The wife who's his companion in joy and sorrow alike.

A mother walks the edge of life to bring her child into the world. For nine long months, she endures pain, sacrifice, and countless silent battles—all to protect the fragile life growing within her, cradling her baby with every heartbeat, even before the world lays eyes on it.

"Congratulations, you have a baby girl," the doctor said.

Chirag hugged the doctor and said, *"I can't put into words how happy I am today. I've been waiting for this good news for years. You are a godsend to me."*

"I only did my duty."

"Doctor, Aashvi is doing well."

"There's nothing to worry about; she's doing fine," the doctor said.

"May I see my wife and daughter?" Chirag asked.

"Some formalities are still being completed, so it will take a little time. Once she is moved to the normal ward, you'll be able to see them," the doctor said.

In one corner of the hospital, a mother lay on the bed with tears of joy glistening in her eyes — silent, grateful tears that only a woman who has carried life within her can truly understand. On the other side, the father was a blur of emotion and energy — sharing the news over the phone with relatives, his voice trembling with happiness, offering sweets to the hospital staff, strangers, anyone who crossed his path.

There was a glow on Chirag's face — a radiant light that hadn't been seen before. It wasn't just happiness. It was fulfilling. It was the look of a man whose heart had been waiting quietly for years… and had finally been heard.

He walked slowly into the room.

The world outside faded away as his eyes fell on the two people who now meant more to him than anything else ever could.

A nurse stood gently holding a tiny bundle wrapped in soft pink — so small, so delicate, yet holding the weight of every prayer they had ever whispered. Beside her, Aashvi rested on the hospital bed, her face pale yet glowing, tired but smiling — the smile of a woman who had fought through pain and fear to bring their miracle into the world.

Chirag took a step forward, his throat tightening, eyes welling up with tears that refused to stay hidden. For a moment, he could only look — overwhelmed, humbled, speechless.

His dream had come true.

Their family was complete.

The nurse placed the baby in his arms — and as he held his daughter for the first time, something shifted within him. A love deeper than words, stronger than time, poured into his soul.

He looked at Aashvi, his voice soft and trembling, "She's perfect… just like her mother."

And in that quiet, golden moment, surrounded by soft beeping machines and the scent of new life, time stood still—for a father, a mother, and the daughter who completed their world.

"Today, I'm incredibly happy. Thanks to you, my family is now complete. Without you, my life would feel incomplete."

"Aashvi, look—her eyes resemble mine, and her nose is a bit like yours."

"Chirag, she's our daughter, so naturally, she looks like us."

"We haven't chosen a name for her yet. If you have any good suggestions, please let us know," Chirag said.

"First, I'll get discharged from the hospital, and then we'll organize a party where the priest will name her."

Epic Party Vibes

In a beautifully decorated garden, everything seemed calm and full of vigor. Among the fresh flowers and soft green leaves, a small bud slowly began to bloom. Its soft petals opened to the morning sunlight, releasing a gentle fragrance that spread through the air, inducing scented pleasantry and calm.

Just nearby, a group of playful sparrows flitted through the branches. They chirped happily, fluttering from tree to tree like little bundles of joy. Their songs filled the air, echoing into the house and bringing with them a soft sense of celebration — as if even the birds knew something special had happened.

And something special did happen.

After years of waiting, hoping, and quietly praying, Chirag and Aashvi's baby girl had finally arrived.

Their little miracle. Their dream come true.

There was giggling in every room. Sweets were being shared with any and every visitor. Calls poured in from excited relatives. Smiles and happy tears were everywhere.
"It's a girl!" Chirag kept saying with a proud smile, his heart so full he could hardly speak.

Soon, it was time to bring their daughter home.

Wrapped in a soft red cloth, the tiny baby looked like a fairy — peaceful and perfect. As Aashvi stepped into the house holding her, something changed. The home that had always been theirs, now felt complete. Warmer. Brighter.

Aashvi's face glowed with joy and relief. Though she was tired, her smile said everything — that this was the happiest moment of her life. In her arms, their daughter slept quietly, unaware of how much love surrounded her already.

Chirag stood nearby, silently watching them both. His eyes were misty, and his hands trembled just a little. This — this right here — was what he had dreamed of for so long. His family. His whole world.

The garden outside still bloomed. The birds still sang. But now, everything felt more alive, more meaningful.

Because a little girl had come home — and with her, she brought a kind of happiness that words could never fully describe.

"Chirag, listen, it's been 15 days, and we still haven't even named our daughter," Aashvi said.

"I was about to discuss this with you as well. Even my colleagues at the office are asking when we're throwing a party," Chirag replied.

"We should organize a small party and invite a few relatives and friends," Aashvi suggested.

"There's an important project going on at the office, so I'll be busy for a few days. Let's organize the party on March 24. You can invite the relatives," Chirag said.

"Where will we organize the party?" Aashvi asked.

"Our home is beautiful, and for a small gathering with just a few guests, there's no place better than our own house. We'll decorate it beautifully, and with God's blessings, everything will go perfectly. You can start making a list of the relatives to invite and the arrangements we'll need," Chirag suggested.

The house stood glowing in celebration, adorned with vibrant marigolds, rose garlands, and flickering lights that danced like little stars. Each corner of the home was touched by color and care, alive with the hum of laughter and the soft clinking of glasses. Guests began to arrive, their joyful chatter adding to the already festive air, as if the walls themselves were smiling.

The moment everyone had been waiting for had finally arrived.

A sense of excitement lingered in the air, warm and electric, like the final note before a song begins. Hearts brimmed with happiness, eyes sparkled with anticipation, and everywhere one looked, there were glimpses of love — in shared glances, warm hugs, and proud smiles.

From the kitchen drifted the mouthwatering aroma of freshly prepared dishes — rich spices, warm breads, and sweet syrups blending into the air like a comforting lullaby. On large silver trays, sweets of every kind — laddoos, barfis, and soft rasgullas — were being carefully arranged, each one a symbol of the sweetness this day had brought into their lives.

And in a quiet room just beyond the noise and cheer, the star of the day was being gently prepared.

The little angel — the one whose presence had changed everything — lay nestled in soft cushions, her tiny face calm and curious. Today, she was being dressed with the greatest care — delicate fabrics in shades of ivory and gold, soft ribbons, and the tiniest jewelry that sparkled like morning dew.

She didn't know why everyone was so excited, but she could feel it — in the way her mother's hands trembled slightly while fixing her little bracelet, in the way her father peeked in every few seconds, just to smile at her.

She looked like a blessing wrapped in grace, a dream brought to life — and on this day, the house, the people, and the hearts within it came together to celebrate her.

It wasn't just an event.

It was a memory being made — one that would be told and retold for years to come, beginning with these words:

"It all started the day our little angel smiled at the world..."

"Chirag, look how adorable our daughter looks," Aashvi said with a smile.

"It feels as if God has sent an angel from heaven just for us," Chirag replied with a heartfelt smile.

Wrapped in a delicate pink dress, soft as a morning light, the little star shimmered like a gem cradled by the universe itself. Every fold of her dress, every blink of her curious eyes, held a magic no one could quite put into words. She didn't need to speak. Her presence alone filled the room with awe.

Guests gathered around her in gentle circles, each one taking their turn to hold her — their hands tender, their smiles genuine. As she passed from one embrace to another, laughter floated through the air, and eyes welled up with emotions that only a child's touch can stir. Her smile, faint and fleeting, curled gently across her tiny lips

Faces flushed with excitement, eyes sparkling with delight—they danced not just with their bodies but with their hearts, caught entirely in the magic of the moment.

Across the room, the adults gathered around tables laden with rich, aromatic dishes. They savored every bite, eyes gleaming with satisfaction, exchanging smiles and stories as the festive music wrapped around them like a warm embrace. Even as they ate, their feet tapped involuntarily, carried away by the infectious rhythm, their enjoyment of the food blending effortlessly with the celebration unfolding all around.

The entire scene was a tapestry of joy, laughter, and togetherness—a beautiful symphony of life in motion. The air was thick with happiness, a celebration not just of a special day, but of hope itself.

And at the heart of it all was the little angel—the embodiment of *Aastha*. In her tiny form lay the promise of a brighter tomorrow, a living symbol of hope that had transformed their family's world forever.

The Journey of Nurturing and Growth

The soft afternoon light spilled through the windows, wrapping the room in a golden glow. A few toys lay scattered on the floor — a plush bunny, a rattle, a stack of colorful rings — all quiet now, as if they too were watching.

Aashvi's eyes lit up, wide with wonder. *"Chirag, look!"* she called out, her voice trembling with excitement. *"Our daughter just took her first step — she's walking now!"*

Chirag turned so fast he almost dropped the cup in his hand. His face lit up with a grin that stretched ear to ear. *"Really? She's walking?"*

"Yes! Look at her!" Aashvi pointed, her heart racing with joy.

And there she was — their little girl, standing in the middle of the room, wobbling slightly, arms out for balance. She took another step, slow and unsure, but determined. Her tiny feet padded across the floor as if she were discovering the world for the first time.

"Wow," Chirag breathed, eyes wide with awe. *"She's amazing."*

The baby let out a bubbly giggle, her face glowing with happiness, as if she knew exactly what she'd just done. Her eyes sparkled with the thrill of it all — the movement, the attention, the excitement of growing.

Aashvi's hand moved to her chest. *"She's growing up so fast,"* she whispered, her voice soft and full of emotion.

Chirag wrapped an arm around her shoulder, never taking his eyes off their daughter. *"Every little step... it's a new chapter,"* he said. *"She's learning the world one step at a time."*

They stood there together, silent for a moment, hearts full, watching their baby girl take another brave step forward — small feet, big milestone.

Aastha was growing — slowly, steadily — like a flower blooming in its own time. With every passing day, her parents watched her change, learn, and discover the world around her. Their days, once predictable, were now filled with laughter, tiny messes, sleepless nights, and the kind of joy that came from simply watching her smile.

Raising a child, they soon realized, was no small journey. It came with its own share of challenges — unexpected, exhausting, yet deeply rewarding. But what struck them most was how naturally their own needs began to shrink in comparison to hers. Their lives, which once revolved around careers, travel plans, and long-forgotten hobbies, now circled entirely around Aastha's tiny world.

They gave — willingly, silently, and completely. Not out of duty, but out of love. Dreams they once chased were now packed away like old photographs, not out of regret, but with the quiet hope that their sacrifices might build a brighter path for their daughter.

In her laughter, they found purpose. In her happiness, they found their own. And though their own ambitions had taken a back seat, their hearts had never been fuller. For nothing compared to the joy of watching their child grow — and knowing they had given everything to see her shine.

Parents are priceless gems,
We must cherish them, it's our duty.
Parents are a support,
Always walking with us, through every pain and worry.

Parents are like raindrops,
They shower us with comfort and peace.
Their blessings, their love,
Always with us, like a journey that never ends.

"It's been such a long time, Aashvi, and we haven't been able to go anywhere because of our little angel," Chirag said, his voice filled with thought. *"I was thinking we should plan a small trip, just to refresh our minds, and it would also be a good chance for our daughter to see some beautiful places. Do you have any place in mind where we should go?"*

Aashvi looked at him, her curiosity piqued. *"Chirag, how much do you love me?"* she asked softly.

Chirag smiled, his eyes shining with affection. *"Seven years of marriage, and our love has already been marked by our little one, who is now two. And you're still asking me for proof of my love?"* he said with a playful tone.

Aashvi smiled, touched by his words. *"My life is yours, I feel so good when I hear you speak about your love for me."*

Chirag, seeing her emotion, continued, *"If that's the case, Aashvi, then listen carefully. Today, I want to tell you something. You are the most beautiful woman in the world to me. Your place is above everything, and I love you more than anything."*

Aashvi looked at him with a hint of challenge in her eyes. *"If you love me that much, then why haven't you shown me a symbol of love yet?"*

Chirag raised an eyebrow, intrigued. *"A symbol of love? What do you mean?"*

Aashvi smiled softly, her voice full of warmth. *"The symbol of love... the Taj Mahal. How can you forget it? It was built by Shah Jahan for his wife Mumtaz. How could you not take me there?"*

Chirag's eyes lit up with excitement. *"How could I forget the Taj Mahal? And I will make sure to fulfill this wish of yours. Tomorrow, we're going on a trip to Agra. Be ready."*

Aashvi's eyes widened with surprise. *"We're going to Agra by car?"* she asked.

Chirag shook his head. *"No, Aashvi. Our Aastha is still small, so we'll take the train to Agra. I'll book the tickets today."*

Aashvi smiled, her heart swelling with love for her husband. *"I can't wait, Chirag."*

Chirag and Aashvi stood on the railway platform, their faces glowing with quiet excitement. It wasn't just another day — it was special. They were about to take their daughter, Aastha, on her very first train ride.

Chirag gently held Aastha in his arms, close to his chest, as if shielding her from the noisy world around them. She was growing so quickly — every day bringing some new word, a new expression, a small surprise. He could feel how much she had changed, even in the smallest ways.

Aastha looked around with wide, curious eyes. Everything was new — the long train tracks, the crowd, the sound of luggage wheels rolling, and the faint whistle of a train approaching in the distance. Her eyes sparkled with excitement, but there was a little shyness too, a quiet hesitation that made her cling just a bit tighter to her father's shirt.

Aashvi stood beside them, watching both of them with a soft smile. She gently brushed a strand of hair away from Aastha's face, whispering something that made the little girl smile.

The train pulled into the station slowly, its rhythm steady and loud. Chirag held Aastha a little tighter, as if to remind her — and himself — that she was safe, no matter how big or new the world felt.

It was a small moment, but it meant so much. For Aastha, it was her first train ride. For Chirag and Aashvi, it was another beautiful first — one of many — in their journey as parents.

With a loving smile, Chirag looked down at his daughter. *"Today is your first journey, little one. This will be a new experience for you,"* he said, his voice full of affection.

Aastha stretched out her tiny hands, fingers fluttering as if trying to catch the wind. She stood close to the edge of the platform, safe in her father's arms, her eyes scanning the tracks with bright anticipation. There was a different kind of energy in her gaze today — curious, alive, almost as if she could sense that something exciting was about to happen. A soft smile tugged at the corners of her lips, the kind that appeared without reason — the way children smile when their little hearts are full of wonder, even before they understand why.

Aashvi, standing beside them, looked at their daughter with love. *"Today is your first train ride, my darling. This will be a memory you'll cherish forever,"* she said softly.

As the sound of the approaching train grew louder, Aastha's face lit up even more. She turned to look at her parents, and Chirag held her more lovingly in his arms. *"Come on, beta, your first train ride is about to begin,"* Chirag said, his voice filled with warmth and pride.

The sound of the train's whistle echoed on the platform, and Aastha's heart filled with joy and anticipation. For her, it was the beginning of a new adventure, and the sparkle in her eyes shone brighter than ever, as if the world itself had just opened up to her.

The train stood waiting at the platform, its engine humming with anticipation as passengers bustled about. Chirag quickly loaded their luggage onto the train, while Aashvi held Aastha close in her arms. Once they settled into their reserved seats on the Rajdhani Express departing from Hazrat Nizamuddin Railway Station, they relaxed and prepared for the journey ahead.

As the train slowly pulled out of the station, it moved with a serpentine grace, picking up speed with every passing second. Aastha, brimming with excitement, stood by the window, her tiny fingers gripping the frame as her wide eyes drank in the sights outside. The city lights flickered and blurred, merging into the silhouettes of distant fields, creating a mesmerizing view for the little one.

By the time the train reached Agra, the evening had set in, and the clock struck 7 PM. The family stepped off the train, greeted by the cool breeze of the historic city. Chirag quickly arranged for a cab, and soon they were enroute to the Radisson Hotel.

The cab driver, a friendly local with a cheerful demeanor, started a conversation. *"Pehli baar Agra aaye hain, saab?"* he asked, glancing at Chirag through the rearview mirror.

"Ji haan," Chirag replied, smiling. *"Hum Taj Mahal dekhne aaye hain."*

"Bahut achha kiya, saab. Taj Mahal subah dekhna sabse accha hota hai. Jab suraj ki roshni Taj ke sangmarmar par padti hai, to lagta hai jaise sona chamak raha ho," the driver said, his voice filled with pride.

"Yeh sunne mein hi kitna sundar lag raha hai," Aashvi said, her eyes lighting up with excitement.

As the cab made its way through Agra's lively streets, the family observed the charm of the city—colorful bazaars, bustling tea stalls, and the glow of evening lights casting long shadows on the historic buildings.

Aastha, tired from the journey, had drifted off to sleep in Aashvi's arms, her small face resting peacefully on her mother's shoulder.

When they reached the gates of the Radisson Hotel, the cab driver smiled warmly. *"Aap log Taj Mahal ka maza lijiye, aur yahan ke Mughlai khane ka bhi. Kabab aur biryani jarur try kariyega."*

"Zarur, shukriya," Chirag replied, paying the fare and thanking him for the advice.

As they stepped into the grand hotel lobby, a soft warmth seemed to wrap around them. Golden lights shimmered overhead, casting a gentle glow across the polished marble floors and elegant furnishings. The quiet hum of distant conversation, the faint scent of fresh flowers, and the calm, inviting atmosphere made the long journey feel suddenly worthwhile.

Chirag walked ahead, rolling their luggage with one hand, his eyes quietly taking in the beauty of the place. Just behind him, Aashvi moved slowly, her arms wrapped protectively around Aastha, who was still fast asleep against her shoulder — her tiny breaths soft and steady.

There was a calm between them — the kind that follows a long trip, but also the quiet thrill of something new. The journey had only just begun, and yet their hearts already felt full. The idea of exploring unfamiliar streets, sharing laughter in cozy cafés, and collecting memories they'd one day look back on — it filled the space between them with a kind of silent joy.

This was more than a trip. It was the beginning of a story they'd tell for years to come.

Chirag and Aashvi stood at the reception desk, where a graceful young woman greeted them with a warm, professional smile.

"Good evening, ma'am," Chirag said politely.

"Good evening, sir," the receptionist replied in a friendly tone. *"How may I assist you today?"*

"We've made an online booking at your hotel," Chirag explained, his voice calm and steady.

"Could you please provide the name under which the booking was made?" she asked, her fingers poised over the keyboard, ready to assist.

"It's under my name—Chirag," he replied. *"The room is reserved for two adults."*

The receptionist nodded, her fingers typing swiftly. *"Let me check… Yes, Mr. Chirag. I see your reservation here. A deluxe room for two adults. Everything is perfectly in order."*

"Thank you," Chirag said with a smile, glancing at Aashvi, who stood beside him, gently rocking Aastha in her arms.

"Welcome to the Radisson Hotel, sir and ma'am," the receptionist said warmly. *"Your room is ready, and I'll arrange for someone to escort you shortly. If you need anything during your stay, please don't hesitate to contact us."*

Moments later, a porter appeared, offering a polite nod before gently taking the luggage and motioning for them to follow. The soft, ambient lighting of the lobby, paired with its tasteful, elegant décor, created a warm and inviting atmosphere that seemed to slow time itself.

Chirag and Aashvi walked behind, their steps quiet, hearts filled. There was a calm sense of comfort in the air — the kind that settles in when you know you're exactly where you're meant to be. With Aastha still sleeping peacefully in Aashvi's arms, and the promise of new memories just beginning to unfold, they felt a quiet excitement stirring within them.

This wasn't just a stay — it was the beginning of a chapter they knew they'd always hold close.

As they stepped into the room, Aashvi's eyes lit up. *"Chirag, what a beautiful room! Look at the two double beds with a table in between,"* she said, her voice filled with excitement.

Chirag smiled, glancing around. *"And look over there,"* he pointed. *"A TV cabinet with a working space. I can even get some office work done here if needed."*

Aashvi raised an eyebrow playfully. *"Did you come here to work, or to spend time with me and enjoy the trip?"*

Chirag chuckled, walking over to her. *"You're my life, Aashvi. I was just admiring the design. Look at how large these windows are!"*

Aashvi laughed softly. *"Come on, let's pull back the curtains and see the view."*

Chirag drew the curtains aside, revealing a scene that was breathtaking. The metro glided silently in the distance, its sleek carriages lit up against the darkening sky. Far beyond, shrouded in the evening haze, the Taj Mahal stood like a dream, its silhouette faint but mesmerizing.

"Aashvi, look at this view," Chirag said, his voice low with awe.

"It's stunning," Aashvi whispered, her eyes fixed on the scene outside. For a few moments, they stood together, quietly taking in the beauty of the city and the timeless monument in the distance.

The room itself was no less impressive. A full-height mirror stood elegantly in the corner, and the bathroom, with its glass walls and sleek fittings, looked straight out of a design magazine. *"Did you see the wardrobe?"* Chirag asked, opening it to reveal ample storage space along with a locker.

"It's perfect," Aashvi said, turning back to look at him, her face glowing with contentment.

Chirag leaned casually against the edge of the bed, a playful smile on his face. *"Aashvi, you're so caught up in your excitement that you forgot Aastha is asleep in your arms. Lay her down on the bed, and hand me my clothes. I'm going to freshen up,"* he said, teasingly.

Aashvi smirked, raising an eyebrow. *"Not so fast, mister. I'm going first, and then it's your turn,"* she replied, carefully placing Aastha on the bed.

Aastha, oblivious to their banter, lay peacefully, her tiny face glowing with the innocence of sleep. Chirag glanced at her and smiled before turning his attention back to Aashvi as she disappeared into the washroom. He waited, sitting on the edge of the bed, drumming his fingers impatiently.

The sound of the washroom door opening caught his attention, and Chirag looked up. Aashvi stepped out, wrapped in a soft towel, another towel draped around her wet hair. Her skin glowed from the warmth of the shower, and tiny droplets of water glistened on her arms.

For a moment, Chirag was captivated, his eyes fixed on her. Aashvi noticed his stare and tilted her head playfully. *"What's wrong, Chirag? Are you seeing me for the first time?"* she teased, her tone light but confident.

"Not the first time," Chirag said, his voice low and filled with admiration. *"But this version of you... it's stunning. I don't think I've ever seen you look this sexy."*

Aashvi laughed, shaking her head as she walked toward the wardrobe. *"A moment ago, you couldn't wait to get into the washroom. What happened to your rush?"*

Chirag stood up slowly, his smirk growing wider. *"The washroom can wait. Right now, I just want to admire my wife."*

Aashvi raised a hand, stopping him mid-step. *"Chirag, behave! Aastha is sleeping right here. Go freshen up before she wakes up,"* she said, her cheeks flushing pink.

Chirag sighed dramatically, running a hand through his hair. *"Fine, fine. But don't think you've gotten away. We'll finish this later,"* he said with a wink, grabbing his clothes and heading toward the washroom.

As the door clicked shut, Aashvi smiled to herself, her heart warm with love. Their playful moments, filled with teasing and affection, made their relationship feel fresh and alive, no matter how busy life got.

In today's fast-moving world, life often feels like a never-ending race — days blurring into one another, each filled with obligations, deadlines, and the constant pressure to keep up. People rush from one task to the next, often unaware of how quickly time slips through their fingers.

And yet, amid all the chaos, there lies a quiet truth: when one pauses, even briefly, to truly cherish their family — to share in laughter, to offer kindness without condition, to show respect in small, everyday ways — those moments take root. They become more than memories. They become anchors.

It is in these simple, heartfelt connections that real happiness lives — not in grand achievements or material success, but in the warmth of togetherness. Such moments, though fleeting, carry a lasting strength. They build bonds that can weather any storm, bringing depth to life and reminding us of what truly matters when the world moves too fast to notice.

There's no denying the importance of earning a living. A steady income, a meaningful career — they bring stability, purpose, and the space to grow. In many ways, they shape the structure of adult life. But somewhere along the way, when work becomes everything, when ambition overshadows affection, a silent cost begins to build — one that isn't measured in money, but in moments lost.

Too many people realize too late that success means little if there's no one left to share it with. Money can buy comfort, even luxury. It can open doors, fund dreams, and offer choices. But it cannot buy time with a loved one. It cannot recreate a child's first steps, a partner's quiet support, or the warm presence of family at the end of a long day.

As someone once wisely said, *"We come into this world empty-handed, and we leave the same way."*

So, what then, is the point of chasing wealth endlessly, if in the process we forget what truly makes life rich — love, connection, and the people who make coming home feel like peace.

Family should always come first. Everything else — success, ambition, wealth — naturally finds its place after that. This isn't to say that one shouldn't work hard or chase dreams; striving for growth is a beautiful part of life. But the key lies in balance — in knowing when to pause, when to listen, and when to simply be present with those who matter most.

Earn well, build the life you've imagined — but not at the cost of forgetting the very people you're building it for. Chasing wealth while neglecting the relationships that give life meaning leads only to a quiet kind of emptiness — the kind that money can't fill.

Because every relationship, every bond worth keeping, survives on time, love, and attention. And in the end, it's not the achievements or the possessions that define a life well-lived, but the moments — however small — spent with family. It's in laughter around the dinner table, the silent support during hard times, the shared joy in everyday things.

That is what stays. That is what matters.

The clock struck ten, its steady chime breaking the quiet of the room. Chirag looked over at Aashvi, who lay stretched out on the bed, her body heavy with exhaustion, every ounce of energy seemingly spent. Her peaceful yet weary expression spoke volumes of the long day she had endured.

"Aashvi, it's already 10. How long are you planning to rest? Don't you want to have dinner?" Chirag asked gently, his voice laced with concern.

Aashvi groaned softly, her eyes barely opening. *"I'm so tired, Chirag. I just want to sleep,"* she murmured, her voice heavy with exhaustion.

Chirag sat down beside her, brushing a strand of hair from her face. *"Come on, Aashvi, have dinner first. The whole night is ahead for you to rest. Eat something, then you can sleep properly,"* he said, his tone calm but firm.

Aashvi let out a small sigh and propped herself up on one elbow. *"Alright, but what about Aastha? Is she awake?"* she asked, glancing toward their daughter, who was peacefully curled up in bed.

Chirag shook his head, a soft smile playing on his lips. *"She's still fast asleep. Wake her up and feed her something too. I'll handle the dinner order,"* he said, picking up his phone.

"Okay," Aashvi said, stretching her arms. *"But what are you planning to order?"*

"What do you feel like eating?" Chirag asked, scrolling through the menu.

"Anything tasty," Aashvi replied, stifling a yawn. *"But no non-veg for me tonight. Keep that in mind."*

"Got it," Chirag said with a nod. *"I'll handle it. You wake Aastha."*

Aashvi smiled faintly as she walked over to their little one. Aastha lay curled up, her tiny fists resting against her cheeks, breathing softly.

"Aastha, my baby, wake up," Aashvi whispered gently, stroking her daughter's soft hair. Aastha stirred, her eyelids fluttering as she slowly opened her big, sleepy eyes.

Chirag looked up from his phone and smiled. *"Perfect timing. She's awake, and dinner will be here soon."*

Aashvi scooped Aastha into her arms, holding her close. *"Come on, my little princess, let's get you something yummy to eat,"* she said, her voice filled with tender affection.

The sound of the doorbell echoed through the room.

"It must be housekeeping with the dinner," Chirag said, getting up to answer the door.

He opened the door to find a polite staff member standing there, holding a trolley laden with food. *"Sir, your dinner is ready,"* the staff member said with a warm smile.

"Bring it in and place it on the table," Chirag instructed, stepping aside.

The staff neatly arranged the dishes on the table—Shahi Paneer, Malai Chaap, Veg Biryani, a fresh salad, butter naan, and a bowl of kheer for dessert. The aroma of the food quickly filled the room, making it feel cozy and inviting.

Aashvi walked over, her eyes lighting up as she took in the spread. *"Wow, Chirag! You've outdone yourself this time. The food looks amazing,"* she said, her excitement evident.

Chirag smiled, pulling out a chair for her. *"Well, my love, you deserve the best. This trip has to be memorable, doesn't it? And good food is a part of making it special."*

Aashvi sat down, laughing softly. *"It's been so long since we've had a trip like this. Ever since Aastha came into our lives, we haven't really traveled anywhere. Remember how much we used to roam around before?"*

Chirag nodded, his smile softening. *"I know, but Aastha brought a new kind of adventure into our lives. And don't worry, we'll make more memories like this, together as a family."*

Aashvi glanced at the table, then back at Chirag. *"Wait a minute, you didn't order anything for Aastha!"* she exclaimed.

Chirag chuckled, reaching for a small bottle from the side table. *"Here's her dinner—warm milk. Our little princess will have her favorite drink while we enjoy this feast."*

Aashvi smiled, taking the bottle and gently waking Aastha. *"Come on, my little angel, it's time for your dinner,"* she whispered.

As Aastha blinked her sleepy eyes open and snuggled into her mother's arms, Chirag served the food, his heart full of quiet joy. This wasn't just dinner—it was a moment of togetherness, laughter, and love, the kind that made life truly beautiful.

Chirag tore off a piece of butter naan, dipped it generously into the rich, creamy Shahi Paneer, and turned to Aashvi with a playful smile. *"Open your mouth, Aashvi,"* he said gently, holding the bite close to her lips.

Aashvi raised her eyebrows in mock reluctance but then smiled softly and opened her mouth. Chirag carefully fed her the bite, watching her reaction with anticipation.

As the flavors melted on her tongue, Aashvi's eyes lit up. *"Mmm, this Shahi Paneer is delicious,"* she said, savoring the taste. She glanced at Chirag and added, *"But you know what? It tastes even better because it came from your hands."*

Chirag chuckled, his gaze warm and affectionate. *"Well, I guess I have the magic touch,"* he teased, breaking off another piece.

The two of them continued to eat, laughing and sharing bites as they relished not just the food but the joy of being together. The room was filled with soft conversation and occasional bursts of laughter, creating a cozy, intimate atmosphere.

They sat close, sharing a quiet dinner that felt more like a celebration than a meal. Laughter danced between mouthfuls, as they playfully offered bites to one another, their eyes meeting often, their smiles saying more than words ever could. It wasn't about the food — it was about this moment, this simple, sacred togetherness.

The soft murmur of their voices, the occasional burst of laughter, and the golden hue of the bedside lamp wrapped the room in a warm, intimate glow. Time seemed to slow down, the outside world gently fading behind the comfort of shared space and unspoken love.

On the bed, Aastha lay nestled against a pillow, her tiny hands clutching her milk bottle. She drank in slow, thoughtful sips, her eyes fluttering between her parents. There was something quiet and knowing in her gaze — as if, even in her tender age, she could feel the warmth that surrounded her.

She watched them in silence, absorbing their joy, the rhythm of their voices, the comfort in their nearness. The room held nothing extravagant — just two tired hearts and one tiny soul — but it was full in the way that only love can make it.

And in that peaceful corner of the world, lit by laughter and lamplight, a memory was quietly being made — one that would stay long after the dishes were cleared and the lights turned off.

Aashvi glanced at her daughter and smiled, her heart full. *"Look at her, Chirag. She's already enjoying this little adventure of hers."*

Chirag turned to see Aastha, her innocent face glowing in the soft light. *"She's the real boss of this trip,"* he said with a grin. *"And we're just here to make sure she has the best time."*

Aashvi laughed, leaning back in her chair. *"I think she's already having the best time, just watching us."*

Chirag nodded, his eyes lingering on his family. *"And I'm having the best time, just being here with both of you."*

The night unfolded with quiet grace — a tapestry of simple joys, unspoken warmth, and the kind of love that turns even the smallest moments into something timeless and grand.

The first rays of dawn spilled gently over Agra, cloaking the city in a golden haze. A soft, almost dreamlike light kissed the rooftops and narrow lanes, giving everything a quiet, otherworldly glow. Morning had arrived not just with light, but with promise.

Inside their hotel room, Chirag and Aashvi moved with a mix of urgency and excitement, their anticipation almost palpable. Today was not just another morning — it was the morning. The one they had waited for. The one whispered about in countless travel tales and echoed in the driver's words from the night before: *"The view of the Taj Mahal in the morning is something truly breathtaking."*

They could still hear his voice in their minds, his tone reverent, as if he spoke of something sacred.

Determined not to miss a single moment of that magic, they moved quickly — packing, dressing, checking the time — yet beneath the rush was a deep stillness, the kind that comes when the heart is full. The image of the Taj Mahal bathed in morning light lived vividly in their imagination, and now, they were just moments away from seeing it with their own eyes.

Outside, the city stirred to life. And within that golden morning, a memory was waiting to be made.

Aastha looked like a little piece of the sky brought to earth — dressed in a soft, sky-blue frock that fluttered gently with her every step. There was an innocent glow about her, as if the morning light itself paused to admire her charm. Her eyes sparkled with wonder, and her bright, effortless smile gave her the presence of a tiny angel — pure, joyful, untouched by the world's rush.

Aashvi, ever graceful, had chosen a timeless look — fitted black jeans and a crisp white top that hugged her slender frame with effortless elegance. Simplicity suited her, and today, it made her beauty shine even brighter.

Chirag, true to his signature style, had dressed in a clean white shirt and black trousers — formal, understated, and refined. It wasn't intentional, but standing beside Aashvi, their matching outfits made them look perfectly in sync — a pair tied not just by color, but by quiet understanding.

The Taj Mahal was just three kilometers from the hotel — a brief journey, yet one that held so much promise. Chirag had already arranged for a cab, and within minutes, the three of them were seated comfortably inside.

As the car pulled out onto the road, there was a quiet excitement in the air — the kind that fills your chest before a long-awaited dream comes to life. Aastha sat between them, her little fingers pressed against the windowpane, eyes wide with curiosity. Aashvi glanced at Chirag, their hands brushing for a fleeting second — a wordless gesture, but filled with meaning.

And so, with hopes in their hearts, light in their eyes, and the warmth of togetherness surrounding them, the three of them set off — toward that eternal symbol of love, known to the world as the Taj Mahal.

The morning breeze slipped gently through the half-open windows of the cab, carrying with it the soft hum of a city slowly waking. Agra stirred quietly — the rustle of leaves, the distant call of birds, the occasional murmur of early risers. The streets, washed in the golden light of dawn, looked peaceful and unhurried, as if the whole city was stretching into the day.

Inside the cab, a quiet excitement was building. The closer they got, the more real it felt — the anticipation of seeing the Taj Mahal, not just as a picture or a story, but with their own eyes. There was something almost sacred in the air, as if time itself had slowed down for this moment.

The cab came to a halt near the parking area, where the buzz of voices drifted in from every direction — a soft mix of different languages, laughter, footsteps. Tourists milled about with cameras in hand, their eyes wide with awe and curiosity.

From there, it was a short walk — five, maybe seven minutes — to the ticket counter. The path ahead was alive with motion. Some people paused to take photos, others simply stood still, quietly amazed, as the iconic white dome of the Taj Mahal peeked through the trees in the distance. It shimmered faintly in the morning light, like a dream slowly coming into focus.

Chirag, Aashvi, and little Aastha walked hand in hand, their steps light, hearts full, and eyes fixed ahead — toward a moment they would carry with them for the rest of their lives.

At the ticket counter, Chirag stood patiently in line. *"Two tickets, please,"* he said as he handed over the cash. Each ticket cost ₹50 for adults, a modest price to witness one of the world's greatest wonders.

He turned to Aashvi, holding the tickets in his hand. *"We've got the tickets. Let's head to the checking area now,"* he said with a smile.

Aashvi matched his pace as they walked towards the checking point, the majestic Taj Mahal drawing closer with every step. *"Chirag, I was thinking, shouldn't we hire a guide? They can explain everything in detail and share the history with us,"* she suggested, glancing at the crowd around them.

"That's a good idea, Aashvi. Let's get one," Chirag agreed.

At the entrance, their tickets were carefully scanned, the faint beep marking their official passage into the historic grounds. Their bags were then thoroughly inspected by the vigilant security staff—no detail overlooked—to ensure the safety of both the visitors and the timeless monument they were about to witness.

Once cleared, they were gently guided to the locker area, a small, orderly space where visitors could securely store their belongings as per the rules. With their bags safely tucked away, a sense of lightness settled over them, allowing them to fully immerse in the magic that awaited beyond.

With everything sorted, they met their guide, a knowledgeable local who greeted them warmly. He carried a small notebook and spoke with an air of enthusiasm.

"Now, let me take you to the main gate of the Taj Mahal," the guide said, leading them forward.

As they approached the grand entrance, their anticipation grew. The main gate, an architectural masterpiece in itself, stood tall and imposing, made of red sandstone adorned with intricate carvings and inscriptions in white marble. The guide paused before the gate, gesturing for them to take in its beauty.

"This," he began, his voice filled with reverence, *"is the Darwaza-i-Rauza, the Great Gate. It symbolizes the passage from the mundane to the eternal, just as the Taj Mahal is a tribute to everlasting love."*

Aashvi and Chirag exchanged a glance, their expressions reflecting awe and excitement. Holding Aastha's hand, they stepped through the gateway, ready to uncover the magic and stories that lay ahead.

Standing at the Darwaza-i-Rauza, the Taj Mahal was still hidden from view, but the grandeur of the gate itself was mesmerizing. The intricate carvings and the magnificent scale of the structure held their gaze. Aastha, with her tiny hands, reached out to touch the smooth surface of the gate, her innocence adding a tender beauty to the moment.

The guide, sensing their awe, began to speak. *"The Taj Mahal, built along the banks of the Yamuna River, is one of the Seven Wonders of the World. It's not just a monument; it's a symbol of eternal love, the undying bond between Emperor Shah Jahan and Mumtaz Mahal. Known as the 'Symbol of Love,' it hosts millions of visitors every year and is a masterpiece of Persian, Indian, Islamic, and European architecture—a rare blend that feels like heaven on earth."*

Chirag, holding Aastha in his arms, listened attentively, while Aashvi stood beside him, her eyes fixed on the guide.

The guide smiled and gestured toward the gate. *"As we step through this gateway, it may feel as though the Taj Mahal is moving farther away from you. This optical illusion was deliberately designed to enhance the awe of the monument. Shall we begin our journey to witness its beauty?"*

Excitement bubbled in their hearts as they walked through the towering gate. And then, there it was—the Taj Mahal, standing in all its splendor, its ivory-white marble glowing under the soft sunlight.

"This is breathtaking," Aashvi whispered, unable to take her eyes off the monument.

Their guide led them to a nearby spot. *"This here,"* he said, pointing to a designated area, *"is one of the best selfie points. Visitors from all over the world stop here to capture their memories with the Taj Mahal."*

Chirag handed his phone to the guide and gently adjusted Aastha in his arms. *"Aashvi, come here,"* he said, motioning for her to join them.

The guide smiled as he took their picture, capturing Aastha's giggles and the joy on her parents' faces. *"This gate,"* he explained, *"is not the main gate but the rear gate of the Taj Mahal. During Shah Jahan's time, four gates were built for entry. This one is called the Fatehpuri Gate, and it's said that Shah Jahan would often come here to view the Taj Mahal."*

As they walked closer to the Taj Mahal, the guide paused and gestured toward the magnificent structure, his voice calm yet filled with reverence.

"During the reign of Shah Jahan," the guide began, *"around 20,000 workers were employed here. Each one of them contributed to this masterpiece, carving and building with unparalleled dedication. If you look up at the grand dome, you'll notice a large finial at the top. It was once made entirely of gold."*

"Gold?" Aashvi asked, her eyes widening in surprise.

"Yes," the guide nodded. *"But during the British era, the golden finial, along with many other treasures inside the Taj Mahal, including precious gems and pearls, was looted and taken away by the British."*

Chirag frowned, looking up at the dome. *"That's heartbreaking. Such a priceless part of history, gone."*

The guide sighed, then continued. *"Mumtaz Mahal, the queen for whom this monument was built, passed away during childbirth. She was giving birth to her 14th child in Burhanpur, a city near the Tapti River. To preserve her body, it was mummified and buried temporarily along the riverbank."*

Aashvi held Aastha a little closer, the story tugging at her heartstrings. *"How devastating it must have been for Shah Jahan,"* she said softly.

"Indeed," the guide agreed, his tone somber. *"Consumed by grief, the emperor issued a decree to build the Taj Mahal as a tribute to her. Six months after her passing, in January 1632, her body was exhumed from Burhanpur and brought to Agra. She was then reburied in the basement of this monument, where she rests to this day."*

The family fell silent for a moment, the weight of the story settling over them.

"Where did they get the materials to build this?" Chirag asked, breaking the quiet.

"The white marble you see came from Makrana in Rajasthan," the guide replied, pointing to the gleaming surface. *"And the red sandstone was brought from Fatehpur Sikri. Every element was carefully chosen, and artisans from all over the world—India, Persia, Turkey, and even Europe—came together to create this masterpiece."*

Aashvi looked at the Taj Mahal with new eyes, her admiration deepened by the story. *"It's not just a monument,"* she said softly. *"It's a testament to love, loss, and the power of remembrance."*

Chirag nodded, holding Aastha's tiny hand. *"And it's a reminder of how far devotion can take someone,"* he said, his voice filled with respect.

The guide smiled, leading them further. *"Come, let's continue. There's still so much more to see and learn about this timeless wonder."*

As they approached the Taj Mahal, its sheer size and elegance became even more breathtaking. The white marble gleamed under the soft sunlight, and its towering structure seemed to touch the sky.

"It looks so magnificent and grand up close," Aashvi said, her voice filled with awe.

Chirag nodded. *"Let's head inside and see what secrets it holds."*

The guide turned to them with a smile. *"To visit the tomb inside, you'll need to pay an additional entry fee of ₹200 per person. Shall we proceed?"*

Chirag handed over the fee, and they followed the guide toward the entrance.

As they walked, the guide gestured toward a large structure nearby. *"This is the mosque,"* he said, pointing to the red sandstone and white marble building. *"It's part of the Taj Mahal complex. On Fridays, the Taj Mahal remains closed to visitors, and prayers are held in this mosque."*

Standing before the mosque, they admired its intricate design. *"It's beautiful,"* Aashvi remarked, running her fingers along the smooth marble.

The guide smiled. *"The symmetry of the Taj Mahal is unparalleled. No matter which angle you view it from, its shape remains perfect."*

As they moved closer to the Taj Mahal itself, the guide continued, *"The tombs you'll see inside are symbolic. The real tombs of Mumtaz Mahal and Shah Jahan lie directly beneath in the basement."*

"Why two tombs?" Chirag asked, intrigued.

"Normally, a mausoleum houses a single tomb," the guide explained. *"But Shah Jahan originally intended to build a black Taj Mahal for himself on the opposite bank of the Yamuna. However, due to various reasons, it was never completed. After his death, his daughters, Jahanara and Roshanara, secretly transported his body from Agra Fort through an underground passage and buried him here beside Mumtaz Mahal."*

"That's such a bittersweet story," Aashvi said, her voice tinged with emotion.

The guide led them further, stopping at the foundation of the structure. *"The Taj Mahal's foundation is built on ebony wood, a type of timber found in southern India. This wood grows stronger with moisture, which is why the proximity to the Yamuna River is so important—it keeps the wood hydrated and the structure stable."*

As they marveled at the monument, the guide pointed to another section of the complex. *"This is the Mehman*

Khana," he said. *"In Shah Jahan's time, royal guests who came to see the Taj Mahal were hosted here."*

Inside the Mehman Khana, the group paused to admire the floral carvings on the walls. Aashvi reached out to touch the intricate designs, tracing the patterns with her fingertips. *"These carvings are so detailed, it's incredible,"* she said softly.

"The Taj Mahal was designed to feel like heaven on earth," the guide said. *"Shah Jahan wanted to create a paradise for his beloved queen, and he succeeded."*

As the tour came to an end, Chirag turned to the guide with a smile. *"Thank you for such an insightful and detailed explanation. It made the visit even more memorable."*

The guide nodded graciously. *"I'm glad you enjoyed it. The Taj Mahal is not just a monument—it's a story, a memory, and a legacy."*

As they stepped out of the Taj Mahal complex, Aashvi looked at Chirag, a hint of fatigue in her voice but a smile still on her lips.

"Chirag, I'm starting to feel hungry. How about we stop at a restaurant for lunch? We can rest a bit before heading to Agra Fort," she suggested, adjusting Aastha's frock as the little one dozed in Chirag's arms.

Chirag nodded in agreement, his smile warm. *"Good idea. A nice meal and some downtime will be perfect before we explore the fort."*

With that, they began walking toward the bustling street, searching for a cozy spot to enjoy a meal and prepare themselves for the next chapter of their journey through Agra's captivating history.

As they stepped into the Royal Dining Restaurant, the warm glow of chandeliers and the soft hum of conversations created a welcoming atmosphere. A polite waiter greeted them with a smile and guided them to a cozy table near the window.

"Welcome, sir and ma'am," the waiter said, handing over the menu card. *"Please take your time and let me know what you'd like to order."*

Aashvi glanced at the menu briefly before looking at Chirag. *"I'm definitely having non-veg today,"* she said with a grin.

"Alright," Chirag replied, scanning the menu. *"Let me see what they have in non-veg dishes."*

The waiter stood attentively as Chirag placed the order. *"We'll have Kadhai Murgh, Butter Chicken, Mutton Rogan Josh, and one Biryani with Butter Naan. For drinks, bring a bottle of mineral water and a Coke."*

Aashvi raised an eyebrow, leaning slightly forward. *"Chirag, you're forgetting dessert,"* she teased.

Chirag laughed, looking at the waiter. *"You heard her. What do you have for dessert?"*

The waiter smiled and suggested, *"For dessert, we have chilled Kesar Kheer and Kesari Shahi Tukda. Would you like to try those?"*

"Perfect," Chirag said, nodding.

"Excellent choice, sir. I'll bring your order in about 30 minutes," the waiter replied, noting everything down before heading off.

As they waited for their food, Aastha sat on a chair beside them, her tiny feet dangling as she curiously observed the people around her. Her eyes sparkled with interest as she watched the waiters move between tables and the diners chatting animatedly.

After a while, the waiter returned with a tray, skillfully arranging the dishes on the table. *"Here's your order,"* he said, placing the steaming Kadhai Murgh, Butter Chicken, Mutton Rogan Josh, and fragrant Biryani in the center, accompanied by Butter Naan and their drinks.

The rich aroma of the food filled the air, making their mouths water.

"This looks delicious!" Aashvi said, her excitement evident.

Chirag smiled as he poured water into her glass. *"It's time to dig in,"* he said, picking up a serving spoon.

The rich aroma of spices filled the air as the meal began. Chirag served a generous portion of Butter Chicken onto Aashvi's plate, while she carefully spooned some fragrant Biryani onto his. Their laughter mixed with the soft clinking of utensils as they enjoyed the delicious spread before them.

"Aashvi, try this," Chirag said, tearing a piece of Butter Naan, dipping it into the creamy Mutton Rogan Josh, and holding it out for her.

Aashvi smiled, leaning forward. *"You're spoiling me today,"* she said softly before taking the bite. *"Mmm, this is amazing. But now it's your turn!"*

She scooped some Kadhai Murgh onto a piece of naan and offered it to Chirag. He leaned forward, savoring the flavors. *"You have good taste,"* he said with a playful grin.

Meanwhile, Aastha sat happily in her high chair, a bowl of chilled Kesar Kheer in front of her. Her tiny spoon moved clumsily but enthusiastically, occasionally spilling a bit onto her bib.

"Aastha loves dessert, doesn't she?" Aashvi said, watching her daughter giggle as she tasted another spoonful of the sweet treat.

"She definitely takes after you," Chirag teased, his eyes twinkling.

Aastha clapped her hands, clearly enjoying the attention and the sweetness of the kheer. The family shared smiles and laughter, the warmth of their bond filling the room as much as the delicious food did.

"Here, one last bite for you," Aashvi said, offering Chirag a piece of Kesari Shahi Tukda.

Chirag leaned in and took the bite, nodding appreciatively. *"You know, this trip is already unforgettable,"* he said, looking at her with a soft smile.

Aashvi returned his gaze, her heart full. *"Because we're together,"* she said simply.

As Aastha giggled, enjoying her dessert, the moment felt timeless—filled with love, laughter, and the simple joys of being a family.

As they finished their meal, Chirag leaned back in his chair, a satisfied smile on his face. He looked at the waiter, who was clearing their table.

"Your food was absolutely delicious. We truly enjoyed it," Chirag said sincerely.

The waiter smiled politely. *"Thank you, sir. I'm glad you liked it. Would you like to have anything else, or shall I bring your bill?"*

"You can bring the bill," Chirag replied, reaching for his wallet.

The waiter returned promptly with a leather folder, placing it gently on the table. *"Here's your bill, sir."*

Chirag opened the folder, checked the amount, and pulled out his card to pay. As the waiter swiped the card, Chirag glanced at Aashvi. *"The food was worth every penny, don't you think?"*

Aashvi smiled, nodding. *"Absolutely. It's been a while since we had such a satisfying meal."*

The waiter handed back the card with a receipt for Chirag to sign. Chirag signed the receipt and, before leaving, took out some cash and handed it to the waiter as a tip.

"Thank you for the excellent service," Chirag said, his tone warm.

The waiter's face lit up with gratitude. *"Thank you so much, sir. I hope you visit us again. Have a wonderful day!"*

As they got up, Chirag picked up Aastha, who was still happily playing with her spoon. Aashvi gathered their belongings, and they made their way out of the restaurant, ready for the next part of their adventure.

After their meal, Chirag booked a cab, and in no time, they were on their way to Agra Fort, covering the short 3-kilometer distance. As the cab stopped, the imposing red sandstone gate of the fort came into view. Its sheer size and grandeur took their breath away.

"Look at this gate, Aashvi," Chirag said, pointing toward the magnificent structure. *"It's so massive. It feels even more majestic than the one at Delhi's Red Fort."*

Aashvi tilted her head, studying the intricate details carved into the gate. *"You're right, Chirag. It's incredible. And see over there,"* she added, pointing toward the deep moat running along the fort's perimeter. *"Imagine how impenetrable this must have been. It's like something out of a storybook."*

Chirag chuckled, admiring her enthusiasm. *"Every inch of this place is built with a purpose. The architecture, the defenses—everything tells a story."*

As they marveled at the structure, Chirag made his way to the ticket counter while Aashvi stayed back with Aastha. The little one clung to her mother's hand, her curious eyes darting from the towering gate to the lively crowd bustling around them.

At the ticket counter, Chirag spoke to the attendant. *"Two adult tickets, please."*

The attendant nodded. *"₹50 per adult. Children under five are free."*

Chirag handed over the cash, collected the tickets, and returned to Aashvi. *"Got the tickets. Ready to go?"* he asked, handing one to her.

Aashvi glanced at the gate again, her excitement evident. *"Ready. Let's step into history,"* she said, holding Aastha's hand as they walked toward the entrance.

As they approached the gate, its towering walls loomed over them, casting a cool shadow. The deep red hues of the sandstone glowed under the afternoon sunlight, making the fort seem alive, almost pulsating with stories of its glorious past.

"Chirag, just imagine the emperors and queens who must have walked through these gates," Aashvi said, her voice filled with awe.

"And now it's our turn," Chirag replied with a smile, gripping Aastha's tiny hand. *"Let's explore this piece of history together."*

With a sense of wonder and anticipation, they stepped through the grand gate, ready to uncover the secrets and stories that Agra Fort held within its timeless walls.

As they approached the grand entrance of Agra Fort, Aashvi gazed at the towering red sandstone walls, her curiosity piqued.

"Chirag," she said, her voice thoughtful, *"let's hire a guide. It made our experience at the Taj Mahal so much more special. I'm sure there's a lot to uncover here too."*

Chirag nodded with a smile. *"You're right, Aashvi. A place like this deserves to be explored with someone who knows its stories."*

Soon, they were greeted by a guide, a man with a warm smile and a wealth of knowledge evident in his demeanor. *"Welcome to Agra Fort,"* he began, his voice steady and engaging. *"This fort has stood witness to centuries of history. It has been ruled by Bharatpur Rajputs, Lodhis, the mighty Mughals, and the Marathas. Finally, the British took control during their conquest of India."*

Aashvi looked around, her admiration for the structure growing. *"It's incredible how much history these walls have seen,"* she said softly.

The guide continued as they walked through the massive gates. *"One of the most poignant stories of this fort is about Emperor Aurangzeb. He imprisoned his father, Shah Jahan, here for eight years. From his confinement, Shah Jahan could only gaze at the Taj Mahal, the symbol of his love for Mumtaz Mahal."*

Chirag sighed, glancing at Aastha, who was clutching his hand. *"That must have been heart-wrenching,"* he said.

Walking deeper into the fort, they reached the Amar Singh Gate. The guide paused. *"This gate is named after Amar Singh Rathore, a brave commander under Shah Jahan. In 1644, he performed an extraordinary feat—leaping from this 75-foot-high gate on horseback. He fought valiantly and helped Shah Jahan win many battles."*

"That's incredible," Chirag said, looking up at the imposing gate with admiration.

They moved on to the Nauwat Khana, where the guide explained, *"This is where returning victorious kings were welcomed with music and dance. Musicians played drums and flutes, and dancers in the jharokhas above showered flowers on the rulers as they entered."*

Aashvi imagined the scene. *"It must have been such a grand celebration,"* she said.

As they continued, the guide led them to a courtyard. *"This is the Akbari Gate. Beyond it lies a gallery where, if enemies ever breached the fort, boiling oil, water, and heavy stones were dropped to stop them."*

Aashvi gasped. *"The level of thought and detail in their defenses is astonishing."*

The guide smiled. *"Come, let me show you something unique."* He led them to a massive stone bathtub. *"This is Jahangir's bathtub, carved from a single stone and weighing 3,000 kilograms. It was gifted to him at birth, filled with jewels and treasures. Jahangir's attendants used this very tub to bathe him as a child."*

"That's amazing!" Aashvi exclaimed, running her hand along the smooth surface.

The guide pointed toward another structure. *"This is Jahangir's Mahal, built by Akbar in Rajasthani and Hindu styles for his son. It's also known as the Rang Mahal because festivals were celebrated here."*

Inside, the intricate carvings and vibrant designs left them speechless. The guide then led them to Jodha Bai's temple. *"Once, this temple housed idols of Radha, Krishna, and other deities. Unfortunately, during Aurangzeb's reign, the idols were removed."*

"It's sad to lose such a connection to history," Aashvi said, her tone reflective.

They passed Akbar's dining hall. *"Here, Emperor Akbar would enjoy his meals,"* the guide said, pointing to an ornate room. *"And through that door is Jodha Bai's kitchen, where she prepared food with her own hands for the emperor."*

As they walked on, the guide pointed to two palaces. *"These belonged to Shah Jahan's daughters, Jahanara and Roshanara. Identical in design, their upper portions were once adorned with gold. Sadly, in 1803, the British looted the gold and replaced it with brass."*

Finally, they reached the Khas Mahal. *"This is the grandest palace in the fort,"* the guide said. *"It was Shah Jahan and*

Mumtaz Mahal's private residence. And there is the Anguri Bagh, where grapes were cultivated. Nearby is the Sheesh Mahal, a masterpiece built by Shah Jahan for Mumtaz. Its mirrored walls reflected light so beautifully that even a single candle could illuminate the entire space."

Aashvi looked around, taking in the beauty and history surrounding her. *"This fort is more than a monument—it's a living story,"* she said, her voice filled with awe.

Chirag smiled, holding her hand. *"And we're lucky to be part of it, even for a day."*

As they left the fort, Aastha giggled, skipping alongside them, her tiny feet echoing against the ancient stone floors. The family walked away, their hearts full of the timeless stories they had uncovered, cherishing the memories they had made.

"Chirag, I'm exhausted," she said with a faint smile. *"I think we should head back to the hotel now."*

Chirag paused for a moment, considering her words. *"I was thinking we could stop by the market for some shopping and then have dinner before heading back,"* he suggested.

Aashvi shook her head gently. *"I don't think I have the energy for shopping right now. And as for dinner, we can just order something once we're back at the hotel. I really need to rest,"* she said, her voice soft but firm.

Chirag gave her a reassuring smile. *"Alright, let's head back. You deserve some rest after such a long day."*

The cab ride back to the hotel was quiet, the city lights flickering past as Aastha dozed off in Aashvi's lap. Chirag glanced at her, noticing the peaceful expression on her face, and felt a sense of calm settle over him.

When they arrived at the hotel, the lobby was softly lit, and the quiet ambiance offered a stark contrast to the bustling streets outside. They made their way to their room, where Aashvi immediately sank onto the plush sofa with a relieved sigh.

Chirag placed their bags aside and sat beside her, stretching his arms. *"Rest for a while, Aashvi. I'll make sure Aastha is comfortable,"* he said, gently laying their sleeping daughter on the bed and tucking her in.

"Thank you," Aashvi murmured, leaning her head back and closing her eyes. *"This day has been amazing, but I really needed this moment of quiet."*

Chirag smiled. *"You rest. I'll handle dinner later."*

The room was filled with a soothing silence, broken only by the soft hum of the air conditioner. The family had shared a day full of stories, history, and wonder, and now they embraced the peace of simply being together. Outside, the city continued its rhythm, but within these walls, time seemed to pause, offering them a sense of serenity and completeness.

The room was shrouded in darkness, the faint hum of the air conditioner the only sound, until Aashvi's panicked voice cut through.

"Chirag! Wake up! Look, Aastha is vomiting!" she cried, her voice trembling with fear as she shook him awake.

Chirag sat up instantly, his heart racing. He leaned over to Aastha, who was coughing weakly. His hand instinctively went to her forehead. *"She's burning up,"* he said, his voice taut with concern. *"And she's had loose motions too. We can't wait—she needs a doctor right now."*

In minutes, they were at the hotel reception, Aashvi clutching Aastha tightly as if afraid to let her go. Her voice cracked as she spoke, *"Please, is there a good hospital nearby? My daughter is very sick—she's been vomiting and has severe loose motions."*

The receptionist quickly responded, his tone calm but urgent. *"Yes, ma'am. Udadhyay Hospital is just 3 kilometers away. I'll arrange for the hotel cab immediately. You'll get there quickly."*

The drive to the hospital was filled with a tense, heavy silence. Aastha lay motionless in Aashvi's lap, her tiny hands limp. Chirag sat beside them, his fists clenched, his mind racing with worry. Aashvi kept glancing at their daughter, tears silently streaming down her face.

When they reached the hospital, Chirag carried Aastha in his arms, walking briskly through the entrance as Aashvi followed, her steps faltering under the weight of her fear. At the reception, he approached a staff member, his voice urgent.

"My daughter is very sick," he said, his words tumbling out. *"She's been vomiting non-stop, and the loose motions won't stop either. Please, help us."*

The receptionist called for a nurse, who arrived quickly. After assessing Aastha, she nodded. *"We'll take her to the emergency room immediately. You both stay here and complete the formalities. We'll examine her and conduct some tests. The ward boy will assist you with the paperwork."*

Aastha was placed on a stretcher, her small frame dwarfed by the sterile white sheets. Aashvi stood frozen, her eyes brimming with tears as she watched their little girl being wheeled away.

"Please," she whispered, her voice breaking. *"Please make her better."*

Chirag touched her arm gently. *"I'll handle the paperwork,"* he said, though his voice wavered slightly. *"You stay here."*

While Chirag dealt with the hospital formalities—signing forms and paying the fees—Aashvi sat outside the emergency room, her hands clasped tightly together in silent prayer. Her tears fell unchecked as she whispered, *"God, please save my daughter. Please, don't let anything happen to her."*

When Chirag returned, he found Aashvi hunched over on the cold metal bench, her shoulders shaking with silent sobs. He sat beside her and placed a comforting arm around her.

"We came here to create memories, Chirag," she said, her voice barely audible. *"I never thought this would happen. If I'd known, I would never have brought her here."*

Chirag sighed, his own emotions bubbling beneath the surface. *"Aashvi, we can't control everything. Whatever happens is in God's hands,"* he said softly, though his eyes betrayed his own fear.

"But why her? Why is this happening to our little girl?" Aashvi cried, her voice breaking as she looked at the closed emergency room doors.

Chirag turned to face her, his expression firm yet gentle. *"I don't know why, Aashvi. But I do know this—if God has given us this trial, He will also give us the strength to overcome it. He is merciful, and He will see us through this."*

Aashvi wiped her tears, nodding weakly, though her heart ached with worry. The minutes dragged on, every second feeling like an eternity. The soft hum of hospital equipment echoed faintly in the background, a reminder of the fragility of the moment.

They sat together, united in their silent prayers, clinging to hope as they waited for news of their daughter, each breath heavy with desperation but anchored in faith.

The emergency room door opened with a faint creak, and a nurse stepped out. Her expression was calm but serious as she approached Chirag and Aashvi.

"The doctor has called for you," the nurse said gently.

Without a word, they followed her down the sterile corridor, their footsteps echoing in the quiet hallway. When they reached the doctor's cabin, Chirag hesitated for a moment before softly knocking and pushing the door open.

"Doctor, may we come in?" he asked, his voice heavy with concern.

The nurse stepped in behind them. *"These are the parents of the little girl who was just brought in,"* she explained.

The doctor looked up from his notes and gestured for them to sit. *"Please, have a seat,"* he said, his tone calm yet professional.

Aashvi couldn't hold back any longer. *"Doctor, what happened to our daughter? Is she going to be okay?"* she asked, her voice trembling.

The doctor folded his hands and leaned forward slightly. *"Your daughter is suffering from diarrhea,"* he explained. *"It's likely caused by something she ate or due to contaminated water. You don't need to worry excessively, but we've had to admit her because she's severely dehydrated and very weak."*

Chirag leaned in, his brow furrowed. *"How long will it take for her to recover?"*

The doctor nodded reassuringly. *"She's already receiving fluids through an IV, and we've started her on medication. With proper care and rest, she should recover soon. But it's essential that you pray for her strength and healing."*

Aashvi's voice was barely a whisper. *"Can we see her?"*

The doctor gave a small smile. *"Of course. The nurse will take you to her room."*

The nurse led them down another corridor to Aastha's room. As they entered, the sight before them was almost too much to bear. Aastha lay on the hospital bed, her tiny frame looking even smaller under the white sheets. Her arm was taped with an IV, the clear fluid dripping steadily into her veins. Her pale face and closed eyes were a stark reminder of her fragile state.

Aashvi gasped, her hand flying to her mouth as tears streamed down her cheeks. *"Chirag, look at her. Look at what she's going through,"* she said, her voice breaking. *"Our little girl… she's in so much pain."*

She began to sob uncontrollably, her shoulders shaking as she gripped Chirag's arm. Chirag wrapped his arm around her, trying to comfort her despite his own anguish.

"Aashvi," he said softly, his voice steady but pained. *"She's strong, and she'll get through this. We have to believe that."*

But Aashvi couldn't stop crying. The sight of her daughter's frail body and the IV needle was too much for her heart to bear.

It was nearing 11:30 PM, and the hospital was silent except for the beeping of monitors. They sat outside

Aastha's room, unable to rest, their eyes fixed on the closed door as if willing it to bring good news.

A nurse approached them quietly, her voice kind. *"I know this is difficult, but pray for her. There's a famous temple nearby, Shri Mankameshwar Temple. It's known for granting wishes. People say that prayers made there are often fulfilled."*

Aashvi looked at the nurse with teary eyes. "You really believe that?"

The nurse nodded. *"I do. My own son was very sick once, and I prayed at that temple. He recovered completely. Sometimes, faith works in ways medicine can't explain."*

Aashvi turned to Chirag, her eyes pleading. *"Chirag, let's go to the temple. Let's pray for Aastha."*

Chirag placed a hand over hers. *"We will, Aashvi, but not now. It's too late. We'll go first thing in the morning,"* he said, his voice soothing.

Reluctantly, Aashvi agreed, and they spent the rest of the night sitting on the chairs outside Aastha's room, unable to sleep. Their eyes remained glued to the door, their hearts heavy with worry and their minds filled with silent prayers. The hours dragged on as they waited, clinging to hope that the next day would bring better news for their precious daughter.

The clock struck 6:00 AM, and the soft hues of dawn began creeping through the hospital windows. Aashvi, her face pale with exhaustion, approached the nurse at the station.

"How is my daughter now?" she asked anxiously, her voice trembling with hope and fear.

The nurse gave her a reassuring smile. *"There's no need to worry. She's doing better than last night. Her condition is stable now."*

Aashvi's eyes glistened with relief as she turned to Chirag, who stood nearby, equally drained but hopeful.

"Let's go see her, Aashvi," Chirag said gently, placing a hand on her shoulder.

But Aashvi shook her head. *"Not yet, Chirag,"* she said firmly. *"First, we need to go to the temple. I made a promise to pray for her recovery, and I won't see her until I've kept that promise."*

Chirag hesitated for a moment before nodding. He could see the determination in her eyes. *"Alright. We'll go now,"* he said softly.

Aashvi turned to the nurse. *"We're going to the temple. Please, take care of my daughter while we're gone."*

"Don't worry," the nurse assured her. *"She's in good hands. You go and do what you need to."*

The morning air was cool as Chirag and Aashvi stepped into the temple courtyard. The sound of bells ringing and the faint murmurs of prayers filled the space. They removed their shoes and climbed the marble steps, their hearts heavy with hope and desperation.

Inside the temple, the idol of the deity stood adorned with flowers and incense, radiating a serene aura. Aashvi folded her hands and knelt before the idol, tears streaming down her face.

"God, please heal my daughter," she whispered, her voice breaking. *"She's our everything. We can't bear to see her in pain. Please, bring her back to us healthy and happy."*

Chirag stood beside her, his hands joined in prayer. His usually calm demeanor gave way to raw emotion as he silently begged for his daughter's recovery. *"She's too little to endure this,"* he thought. *"Please, show your mercy."*

For a long moment, they remained there, their heads bowed, their whispered prayers mingling with the sound of the temple bells. Aashvi placed her forehead on the cool marble floor, surrendering herself completely to her faith.

After lighting a diya and offering flowers, they made their way back to the hospital, the weight in their hearts slightly lighter, their hope renewed.

As they entered the hospital, the nurse greeted them with a smile. *"She's awake now,"* she said warmly. *"You can see her."*

Aashvi and Chirag exchanged a glance, their steps quickening as they made their way to Aastha's room. Opening the door, they saw their daughter sitting up weakly on the bed, her tiny hand clutching the corner of the blanket. Her face was pale, but her eyes lit up when she saw them.

"Papa, Mama," she said softly, her voice weak but filled with warmth.

Tears welled up in Aashvi's eyes as she rushed to her daughter's side, enveloping her in a gentle hug. Chirag sat on the edge of the bed, holding Aastha's hand.

"You're so brave, my little girl," he said, his voice choked with emotion.

Aashvi kissed Aastha's forehead, her heart swelling with gratitude. *"God has listened to us, Chirag,"* she said, her voice trembling with relief.

For the first time in what felt like an eternity, the weight of worry lifted, replaced by a sense of peace as they sat together, grateful for the precious gift of their daughter's recovery.

As the afternoon sun streamed through the hospital windows, Chirag approached the nurse with a question that had been on his mind all day.

"When will Aastha be discharged?" he asked, his voice filled with both hope and concern.

The nurse offered a kind smile. *"The doctor examined her earlier and said she's recovering well. If everything stays stable, we'll discharge her by this evening. But you'll need to take extra care of her—she's still very weak."*

Chirag nodded. *"Thank you. We'll make sure she gets the rest and care she needs."*

Later, as he returned to Aashvi, who sat by Aastha's bedside, he spoke softly. *"Aashvi, let's book our tickets for Delhi. We need to take her home where she can recover properly."*

Aashvi gently stroked Aastha's hair, her gaze not leaving her daughter's peaceful face. *"That's a good idea, Chirag. But let's not travel tonight. She's too fragile, and I don't want to move her during the night. We can rest at the hotel tonight and leave for Delhi in the morning by cab."*

Chirag sat beside her, nodding in agreement. *"That makes sense. I've already informed our parents. They've been so worried. I told them we'll reach Delhi by tomorrow afternoon, and they're planning to come from Rajasthan to see Aastha by the evening."*

The hours passed slowly, and soon the doctor confirmed Aastha was ready to be discharged. Chirag completed the formalities, and by dusk, they left the hospital, with Aashvi carrying Aastha in her arms.

As they drove back to the hotel in the quiet of the evening, Aashvi held Aastha close to her chest. The rhythmic hum of the car seemed to lull her into a deeper sleep. Aashvi's eyes glistened as she gently kissed her daughter's forehead.

"She looks so calm now," Chirag said softly, glancing at them from the front seat.

"She's been through so much," Aashvi replied, her voice heavy with emotion. *"I just want to get her home and make her feel safe."*

When they reached the hotel, the staff greeted them kindly, helping with their belongings. Chirag carried their bags while Aashvi cradled Aastha protectively, her steps steady despite her exhaustion.

In their room, the soft lighting and familiar comfort brought a sense of relief. Aashvi laid Aastha gently on the bed, tucking her in carefully. The little girl stirred slightly but remained asleep, her face peaceful.

"She needs all the rest she can get," Aashvi murmured, her voice tender as she adjusted the blanket.

Chirag stood by the window, staring at the city lights twinkling in the distance. *"This trip didn't go as we'd planned,"* he said quietly. *"But it's reminded me of what truly matters."*

Aashvi walked over, placing a comforting hand on his arm. *"She's safe now, Chirag. That's all that matters,"* she said softly.

The evening air was cool and carried with it the faint, comforting aroma of chai from a nearby stall, wrapping the railway platform in a nostalgic warmth. Chirag stood there quietly, the soft murmur of the bustling crowd fading into the background as his gaze remained fixed on the empty tracks stretching ahead. Every moment felt heavy with longing.

He was waiting for his parents—their journey to Delhi filled with hope and love, all for their precious granddaughter, Aastha.

Chirag had arrived in the city earlier that afternoon with his own family, their hearts weighed down by worry for the little girl they cherished so deeply. Now, as the distant rumble of the approaching train grew louder, a flutter of anticipation stirred within him. It had been so long since he had last seen his parents, and in this moment, their presence felt like a lifeline—something to hold onto amid the uncertainty.

The platform, the evening, even the faint scent of chai—it all seemed to hold its breath with him, waiting for the moment when they would finally reunite.

The rhythmic clatter of the train grew louder, and soon it emerged from the distance, its headlights piercing through the fading light of dusk. Chirag's gaze followed its approach, a mix of emotions playing across his face. Relief, longing, and a deep need for comfort filled his heart.

Life has a way of reminding us of the people who truly matter during moments of uncertainty. When we face unforeseen challenges, the presence of our loved ones becomes a lifeline—a source of strength and solace.

For Chirag, the past few days had been overwhelming. Aastha's sudden illness had shaken him, leaving him feeling vulnerable and helpless. His parents, sensing his struggle, had decided to travel immediately to be by his side.

Parents have an unspoken understanding of their children's pain. They know when their child needs them, even if no words are spoken. Chirag's parents understood his turmoil without him having to say a word.

As the train screeched to a halt and the doors opened, Chirag's eyes scanned the crowd until he saw them. His father, with his calm demeanor, and his mother, her face lit with concern and warmth, stepped onto the platform. Chirag's heart tightened at the sight of them.

"Beta," his mother called out, her voice cutting through the noise of the bustling station.

Chirag quickly moved toward them, his steps eager. When he reached them, his mother pulled him into a tight embrace, her hands gently patting his back as if trying to absorb his stress. His father placed a firm hand on his shoulder, offering silent reassurance.

"How is Aastha now?" his father asked, his tone steady but filled with concern.

"She's better," Chirag replied, his voice catching slightly. *"But she's still weak. I'm just so relieved you're here."*

His mother cupped his face, her eyes scanning his features as if searching for signs of hidden pain. *"We're here now, beta,"* she said softly. *"Everything will be okay. You've been so strong for your family. Let us take care of you now."*

Chirag nodded, a wave of emotion crashing over him. In that moment, he realized how much he had missed their comforting presence, their ability to make even the heaviest burdens feel lighter.

As they walked together toward the station exit, Chirag felt a sense of calm wash over him. The road ahead still held challenges, but with his parents by his side, he felt less alone. Sometimes, the simple presence of family is all it takes to rekindle hope and remind us that, no matter how difficult life gets, we are never truly alone.

As Chirag and his parents entered the house, an almost unbearable heaviness hung in the air. The home, once filled with laughter and warmth, now seemed subdued and lifeless, weighed down by days of worry and uncertainty. Near the doorway stood Aashvi, her face pale, her eyes swollen from countless sleepless nights and tears. As she saw Chirag's parents step inside, her lips quivered.

"Papa, Maa," she said softly, her voice cracking as she approached them.

Chirag's mother immediately moved toward Aashvi, taking her hands in hers. *"Aashvi, how are you holding up?"* she asked, her own voice trembling with concern.

Aashvi shook her head, unable to form the words. *"Aastha... she's still so weak,"* she finally whispered, tears spilling over.

Chirag led them to Aastha's room. The little girl lay on the bed, her small frame almost swallowed by the soft blankets. Her face was pale, her eyes closed, and her tiny hand rested limply on the pillow. The IV needle in her arm and the soft hum of the portable medical equipment made the sight even more heartbreaking.

Chirag's mother gasped, her hands flying to her mouth. *"My granddaughter..."* she murmured, her voice breaking as tears streamed down her face. She moved to the bed, sitting gently beside Aastha, afraid to disturb her fragile state.

Chirag's father stood at the doorway, his expression unreadable yet deeply pained. He placed a firm hand on Chirag's shoulder, squeezing it lightly. *"She's so small... so innocent,"* he murmured, his voice heavy with emotion. *"To see her like this... it's unbearable."*

Aashvi knelt beside the bed, taking Aastha's hand in hers. Her fingers trembled as she stroked the back of her daughter's tiny palm. *"I don't know what else to do,"* she said, her voice shaking. *"I've prayed, I've done everything, but she's still so weak. What if—"* Her words caught in her throat, and she buried her face in her hands, sobbing uncontrollably.

Chirag immediately knelt beside her, wrapping his arms around her in a protective embrace. *"Aashvi, listen to me,"* he said, his voice steady despite the emotion threatening to spill over. *"She's going to get through this. She's stronger than we think. We just need to stay strong for her."*

Chirag's mother leaned over, gently brushing Aashvi's hair back. *"Beta,"* she said softly, her voice filled with warmth and empathy. *"You've been so brave, but you're not alone anymore. We're here now. We'll face this together."*

Aashvi lifted her tear-streaked face, meeting her mother-in-law's gaze. Her lips quivered. *"I just want her to smile again,"* she whispered.

Chirag's father stepped closer, his voice firm yet kind. *"And she will,"* he said. *"But she needs you both to hold on. She needs your strength to fight through this."*

The family gathered around Aastha's bed, their shared silence heavy with unspoken fears but also glimmers of hope. Chirag's mother gently caressed Aastha's forehead, her touch tender and full of love. *"My little angel,"* she murmured, *"you're going to be okay. We're all here with you. You're not alone."*

Aastha was slowly finding her way back to health, cradled in the tender care of those who loved her most. Surrounded by her parents and grandparents, each moment became a gentle step toward recovery. The house—once clouded by silence, worry, and sleepless nights—had begun to shift. Now, it pulsed softly with warmth, like a sanctuary where love itself was the medicine.

Each day, her parents and grandparents moved around her with quiet devotion, taking turns sitting by her bedside. Whether it was adjusting her pillow, stroking her hair, or simply holding her tiny hand, they did it with the kind of patience and presence that only comes from deep, unwavering love. No word was spoken in haste, no task done without care.

In that cocoon of togetherness, Aastha's laughter slowly returned — faint at first, like a forgotten melody — but growing stronger with each passing day. And with it, the light in their lives began to glow once more.

Echoes of Birthday Celebration

The evening sun poured a soft golden glow across the living room, stretching long shadows along the walls. Aashvi gently set a steaming cup of tea on the table and settled next to Chirag on the sofa, her mind clearly wandering somewhere far away. In the corner, little Aastha was busy with her toys, her laughter ringing out like a sweet melody — a sound so rare and precious, it felt like they hadn't heard it in forever.

"Chirag," Aashvi began, her voice soft but purposeful, *"our little girl is finally healthy again. And day after tomorrow, it's February 21—her birthday."*

Chirag looked up from his tea, his expression brightening. *"You're right," he said, a gentle smile spreading across his face. "She'll turn five. I almost can't believe it."*

Aashvi leaned forward slightly, her hands clasped together. *"I was thinking we could make it really special this year. In the morning, we could start with a havan and pooja to thank God for her recovery. And in the evening, we could celebrate her birthday with a party. What do you think?"*

Chirag set his cup down, nodding in agreement. *"That's a beautiful idea, Aashvi. Aastha's been through so much, and this would make her feel loved and cherished. It's perfect."*

Aashvi's eyes sparkled with anticipation. *"And it'll mean so much to our parents too. They've been here for her—and for us—every step of the way. They'll love being part of the celebration."*

Chirag glanced at Aastha, who was carefully arranging her toys in a straight line. A soft smile tugged at his lips. *"She's growing up so fast. I can't believe she's going to be five. Now that she's healthy again, we really need to think about her admission. We've already delayed it too long."*

Aashvi chuckled lightly, her tone affectionate. *"We'll talk about that after her birthday. Right now, I want to focus on making this day perfect for her. It's not just her birthday—it's a celebration of her health, her happiness, and our gratitude."*

Chirag reached for her hand, his touch warm and steady. *"You're right. She's our little miracle. Let's make it a day she'll always remember."*

They sat together, planning every detail—the decorations, the guest list, the food. Chirag volunteered to take care of the cake, which earned him a playful smile from Aashvi.

"You always think of the cake first," she teased.

"Of course," Chirag replied with a grin. *"It's the centerpiece of any celebration."*

They both turned to watch Aastha, who was softly humming to herself, completely lost in her own little world, unaware of the loving plans being woven around her. Her innocent smile, her carefree spirit—it was as if time had paused just to hold that perfect moment. Seeing her so pure and joyful filled their hearts with a gentle warmth that words could never capture.

As the evening deepened and shadows grew longer, the house hummed quietly with a special kind of excitement. This wasn't just a celebration of a birthday; it was a tribute to the unbreakable bond of their family, the love that had carried them through every hardship, and the incredible strength of their little girl who had faced so much and emerged shining brighter than ever.

The living room was calm, the soft evening light casting a gentle glow as Chirag sat with his parents.

"Mom, Dad," Chirag began, breaking the silence. *"Day after tomorrow is Aastha's birthday."*

His mother's face brightened instantly. *"How could we ever forget our little angel's birthday?"*

Chirag smiled faintly and continued, *"We were thinking of starting the day with a small prayer ceremony to thank God for her recovery, and in the evening, we could have a simple celebration. I wanted to check with you both first."*

His father leaned forward, nodding in approval. *"That's a wonderful idea. It's the perfect way to celebrate her health and bring happiness back to the house."*

His mother added, her voice warm, *"Aastha will be so happy. This will make her feel so loved and cherished after everything she's been through."*

Chirag felt a wave of relief and gratitude wash over him. *"Thank you. Let's make this day truly special for her."*

The day they had long awaited had finally arrived, wrapped in a gentle buzz of anticipation and joy. The house had transformed overnight into a vibrant sanctuary, where colorful balloons swayed lightly in the breeze and fresh flowers scattered their sweet fragrance into every corner. The air was alive with laughter and soft conversations, as guests began to trickle in, their bright smiles weaving a comforting warmth through the festive atmosphere.

On the rooftop, a sacred space had been carefully prepared for the havan. At its heart, a holy fire flickered softly, its golden flames dancing gracefully to the rhythm of the gentle morning breeze. Around the fire, family and friends gathered in a calm, reverent circle. The serene chants of the pandit floated through the air, filling the space with an aura of peace, devotion, and timeless spirituality.

Chirag sat with Aastha in his lap, holding her small hand gently as she gazed at the flickering fire with wide, curious eyes. In her tiny hand, she clutched a small silver spoon, dipping it into a bowl of ghee as guided by Chirag. With each chant, she poured a few drops into the sacred fire, her innocence adding a purity to the ritual that made everyone's hearts swell.

Aashvi sat beside them, her hands folded in quiet reverence. Her face, though calm, reflected the gratitude and joy she felt in that moment. After all the challenges they had faced, this ceremony felt like a new beginning—a prayer for their little girl's health and happiness.

As the pandit continued reciting the mantras, the atmosphere grew even more divine. The rhythmic sound of the chants, the crackling of the fire, and the faint aroma of incense wove together, creating an aura of sanctity.

Finally, the havan reached its conclusion. The pandit gestured to Chirag and Aashvi to bring Aastha closer. He took a small pinch of red vermillion and gently applied a tilak on Aastha's forehead, his gaze kind and full of blessings.

He then smiled at Aastha, taking her into his arms briefly as he offered her a small piece of prasad. "*Beti*," he said warmly, his voice resonating with sincerity, "*may the divine always protect you, may every difficulty stay far from you, and may you achieve great success in life."*

Aastha looked up at him with her bright eyes and smiled softly, her innocence lighting up the moment. Chirag and Aashvi exchanged a glance, their hearts brimming with gratitude and pride.

The pooja had been perfect, a deeply meaningful ritual that brought everyone together in prayer and celebration. The family sat together for a moment longer, soaking in the peace and happiness that filled the air, ready to step into the rest of the day with joy in their hearts.

The house was alive with excitement, adorned in vibrant hues of flowers and colorful balloons. Their gentle fragrance mingled with the cool evening breeze, filling the air with a sense of joy and celebration.

Guests began arriving steadily, their cheerful chatter weaving through the melodic hum of soft background music. In the garden, everything had been arranged meticulously. One side boasted an elaborate spread of food, its mouthwatering aroma wafting through the air, while the other held a beautifully decorated table reserved for the evening's main event—the cake cutting.

As the sun dipped below the horizon, the entire house and garden lit up in a cascade of colors. Strings of twinkling lights shimmered against the darkening sky, transforming the space into an enchanting wonderland. Chirag and Aashvi watched the preparations with pride and relief.

"*Chirag, is everything ready?"* Aashvi asked, her voice tinged with excitement and nervousness.

He nodded with a reassuring smile. *"Yes, everything's in place. Dad and I double-checked everything earlier. With God's blessings, tonight will be perfect."*

She gave a small nod, her gaze drifting to the vibrant decor, where every corner radiated happiness and warmth. Guests, dressed impeccably, trickled in, carrying gifts and bouquets for the evening's star—Aastha.

As the clock struck seven, it was time for the cake-cutting ceremony. Aastha, dressed in a soft pink frock adorned with tiny sparkles, stood near the table, wide-eyed and brimming with excitement. The table held a magnificent three-tiered cake, lovingly chosen to match her favorite colors. Aashvi and Chirag guided her tiny hands as she held the silver knife, and together, they cut through the first slice.

The crowd erupted into a harmonious chorus:

"Happy birthday to you,
Happy birthday to you,
Happy birthday dear Aastha,
Happy birthday to you!"

Laughter rang through the air like music as Aastha giggled joyfully, clapping her tiny hands in rhythm with the room full of cheers. Her eyes sparkled with pure delight, and her face glowed with the kind of happiness only a child can radiate. With adorable concentration, she took small slices of cake and fed them—one by one—to her grandparents, parents, and the loving uncles and aunts who had gathered around her. Each gesture brought wide smiles, and in every pair of eyes, her joy was reflected like sunlight in still water.

As the cake-cutting ceremony continued, the gentle background music gave way to a livelier tune. The soft beats turned playful, and a ripple of energy swept through the crowd. The guests, now fully immersed in the celebration, made their way to the dance floor with laughter and light footsteps.

Chirag's friends, grinning from ear to ear, nudged each other as they approached him with that familiar twinkle of mischief in their eyes—ready to pull him into the fun, whether he liked it or not.

The evening shimmered with togetherness—of shared memories, dancing lights, and the kind of happiness that leaves behind a glow long after the music fades.

"Chirag, today's a big day for you," one of them teased. *"You can't escape dancing with Aashvi this time!"*

Caught off guard, Chirag chuckled. *"Alright, alright! But don't blame me if she's the one who refuses."*

He turned to Aashvi, who was busy ensuring the guests were comfortable. Taking her hand gently, he led her to the center of the stage.

"Chirag!" she whispered urgently. *"What are you doing? Everyone's watching!"*

He smiled, unfazed. *"And why not? Let them watch. After all, you're the queen of my heart."*

Before she could protest, the music swelled around them.

"Tere haath mein mera haath ho,
Sari jannatein mere saath ho,

Tu jo paas ho phir kya yeh jahaan,
Tere pyar mein ho jaaun fanaa..."

Their movements were slow and tentative at first, but soon, they found themselves lost in the moment. The crowd erupted into cheers and claps as the couple swayed to the melody, their love reflected in their every step.

Suddenly, a small voice broke through the music. *"Papa!"*

Aastha had toddled onto the stage, her tiny arms outstretched toward Chirag. He bent down, scooping her into his arms with a wide grin.

"Everyone, a moment of silence!" he announced, raising a hand. *"This dance was for my beautiful wife, but now, I dedicate the next moment to the light of our lives—our little angel, Aastha."*

As the crowd cheered, Chirag called for a microphone. With Aastha nestled in his arms, he began singing in a rich, heartfelt voice:

"Tujhko Na Dekhu To Jee Ghabrata Hai,

Dekh Ke Tujhko Dil Ko Mere Chain Aata Hai,

Yeh Kaisa Rishta Hai Kaisa Naata Hai,

Har Gham Utha Loon Tanha Akela,

Tere Liye Hai Khushiyon Ka Mela,

Saara Sansaar Doon Jeevan Bhi Vaar Doon,

Jitna Kahe Tu Utna Main Pyaar Doon,

Yeh Tera Mukhda Hi Mujhko Bhaata Hai,

Dekh Ke Tujhko Dil Ko Mere Chain Aata Hai..."

The melody floated through the night air, soft and stirring, touching every soul present. It carried more than music—it carried emotion, memory, and the silent language of love. As Aashvi watched the two people she held dearest—Chirag and little Aastha—her eyes shimmered with unshed tears. There was a tenderness in the moment that words could never capture. Even the most stoic among the crowd found themselves blinking back emotion, overwhelmed by the raw, unspoken beauty of the scene.

When the final note faded into the night, the garden erupted in applause—loud, heartfelt, and thunderous. It echoed off the walls and into the sky, wrapping the moment in celebration. Aastha, her eyes bright with excitement, clapped her tiny hands with all the joy and innocence of childhood, her laughter spilling into the air like sunlight through leaves.

Guests hurried toward the stage, surrounding her with blessings, gifts, and unfiltered affection. One by one, they lifted her into their arms, showering her with love as she giggled, eyes wide with delight, basking in the warmth of the attention.

As the stars climbed higher into the night sky, the celebration flowed effortlessly into a grand dinner. Plates were filled with delicious food, but more importantly, the tables overflowed with laughter, stories, and the quiet comfort of togetherness.

It was a night that didn't need grandeur to be grand. A night where love had taken center stage—unapologetic and glowing. A night to honor a little girl who had unknowingly brought an entire family, and even strangers, closer to each other.

Later, as the last guests hugged goodbye and the garden quieted, the family remained. Together, they stood beneath the blanket of stars, holding hands, hearts full. And in that silence, one truth settled deep within them—this was a day they would carry with them forever, etched into the folds of memory, where only the most beautiful moments reside.

A New Dawn: The First Day of School

The entire family was busy preparing for Aastha's school admission interview. Now that she had turned five, it was time to take the first step toward her education. Excitement and nervousness filled the air as everyone wanted the best for her.

"I was thinking of enrolling her in Delhi Public School," Aashvi said, looking at Chirag as she flipped through a list of schools.

Aashvi frowned. *"She's our only daughter, Chirag. Everything we have is for her. Don't you want to give her the best future possible?"*

"It's not that, Aashvi," Chirag sighed. *"There will be more expenses in the future—her higher education, and eventually, her grand wedding. We need to start saving now."*

Aashvi's eyes darkened with determination. *"We will raise our daughter in a way that she won't need anyone to spend on her wedding. She will be strong, independent, and capable of choosing her own life partner."*

Chirag saw the fire in her eyes and knew there was no room for further argument. He smiled, nodding.

"Alright," he said. *"Aastha will study at Delhi Public School."*

Aashvi's face broke into a victorious smile. *"Now that's a decision I can stand by. Let's get her ready for the interview."*

The tension in the room lifted, replaced by excitement. Aastha's journey was about to begin, and her parents were ready to give her the best start possible.

Aastha sat between her parents in the waiting area of Delhi Public School, her tiny fingers wrapped tightly around Aashvi's hand. The hallway buzzed with hushed whispers and the quiet murmurs of other parents and children, all waiting anxiously for their turn. Despite the comfortable seating and cheerful decor, a palpable tension lingered in the air.

Chirag and Aashvi exchanged nervous glances. This wasn't just an interview—it was the first step toward securing their daughter's future. They had dreamed of enrolling her in DPS, and after weeks of preparation, the moment had finally arrived. Aashvi had meticulously trained Aastha, ensuring she could introduce herself with confidence, answer basic questions, and maintain a polite demeanor. But what if she got nervous? What if she forgot everything? The thought of failure was unsettling.

Just then, a poised woman entered the room, her elegant saree draping flawlessly over her slender frame. She exuded an air of authority and warmth as she glanced at the clipboard in her hands.

"Aastha?" she called, scanning the room.

Chirag immediately rose from his seat. *"Yes, she's Aastha, my daughter,"* he responded with a polite smile.

The woman returned the smile and nodded. *"You've applied for LKG admission, correct? As per our school policy, this session includes an interaction with both the child and the parents."* She gestured towards the door. "Please follow me."

Aastha hesitated for a brief moment before gripping Aashvi's hand tighter. Sensing her apprehension, Aashvi gave her a reassuring squeeze. Together, they stepped forward, crossing the threshold into the interview room—a space that held the key to Aastha's future.

The interview room was bright and inviting, with colorful posters of alphabets, numbers, and cheerful cartoon characters adorning the walls. A small bookshelf filled with children's books sat in one corner, and in the center of the room, a neatly arranged table awaited them.

Aastha hesitated for a moment as she stepped inside, looking up at Chirag and Aashvi for reassurance. Chirag gently patted her head while Aashvi gave her a soft smile.

Behind the desk sat the same elegant woman who had called Aastha's name earlier. She introduced herself with a warm smile, *"Good morning! I am Mrs. Khan, the admission officer. Please, have a seat."*

Chirag and Aashvi sat down, and Aastha climbed onto the chair beside them, her small legs dangling above the floor. Mrs. Khan turned her attention to Aastha and spoke gently.

"So, Aastha, tell me, what is your full name?"

Aastha glanced at her mother before answering in a soft but clear voice, *"Aastha Mehra."*

Mrs. Khan nodded approvingly. *"That's a lovely name! And how old are you?"*

"I am five years old," Aastha replied confidently.

"That's wonderful! Do you know any rhymes?"

Aastha's face lit up. She straightened her posture and began,

"Twinkle, twinkle, little star,
How I wonder what you are!"

Her sweet voice filled the room, and Mrs. Khan clapped softly when she finished.

"Well done, Aastha! Now, tell me, what is your favorite color?"

"Pink!" Aastha said excitedly.

Mrs. Khan smiled and nodded. *"That's a beautiful color. And what do you like to do in your free time?"*

"I like to draw and play with my dolls," Aastha answered.

"That sounds like so much fun! Now, can you tell me the name of the place where you live?"

"Delhi," Aastha replied, her voice steady.

"Excellent!" Mrs. Khan then turned to Chirag and Aashvi. *"You have trained her well. She is confident and well-mannered, which is always a good sign. Now, I'd like to ask you both a few questions."*

Chirag straightened in his chair, while Aashvi smiled, ready to answer.

"What are your expectations from the school?"

Chirag spoke first. *"We want Aastha to receive quality education in a nurturing environment. We believe in holistic learning, where she can grow academically and socially."*

Aashvi added, *"We also hope she develops good values, discipline, and creativity. DPS is known for its balanced approach to education, and we would love for Aastha to be part of this institution."*

Mrs. Khan nodded. *"That's great to hear. Education is a shared responsibility between parents and teachers, and it's always wonderful to see parents so involved."*

She looked back at Aastha and said, *"You did a fantastic job today! I am very happy to have met you."*

Aastha beamed with pride, looking at her parents, who were equally relieved and proud.

Mrs. Khan stood up and shook hands with Chirag and Aashvi. *"We will inform you about the results soon. But I must say, Aastha is a bright and delightful child."*

As they stepped out of the room, Aashvi let out a deep breath. Chirag smiled at her. *"She did amazing,"* he whispered.

"Yes," Aashvi agreed, looking at Aastha, who was skipping happily beside them. *"Our little girl is growing up."*

"Aashvi, listen!" Chirag's excited voice echoed through the house.

Startled, Aashvi rushed towards him. *"What happened, Chirag? Why are you shouting?"*

"Aastha's result is out!" Chirag announced, his fingers tapping rapidly on the laptop keyboard. The Delhi Public School (DPS) website was open, and the admission result list was displayed on the screen.

Aashvi's heart pounded. *"What does it say? What about Aastha?"*

Chirag's face lit up with joy as he pointed to the screen. *"She got selected!"* His voice was filled with excitement.

"Move aside, let me check!" Aashvi leaned in, scanning the list.

Chirag chuckled. *"What is there to check? Look! Here's her name!"* He pointed at the screen again.

Aashvi's eyes widened with happiness. She read Aastha's name twice, as if making sure it was real. Then, unable to contain her emotions, she turned to Chirag, her eyes glistening.

"Our Aastha is going to DPS!" she whispered, her voice trembling with joy.

Chirag pulled her into a tight hug. *"Yes! Our dream has come true!"*

Without wasting another second, Aashvi grabbed her phone and dialed her parents. The moment they answered, she exclaimed, *"Papa! Aastha got admission into DPS!"*

Her father's voice boomed with happiness. *"That's wonderful news, beta! I am so proud of her!"*

"We should distribute sweets!" her father said.

"Yes, Papa! Chirag is already on it!" Aashvi laughed, watching her husband hurriedly open a box of sweets for their building's security guard.

Meanwhile, Chirag was busy collecting all the necessary documents for the admission process. *"We need to get everything ready, Aashvi. Tomorrow, we complete the formalities."*

Aashvi nodded, wiping away a happy tear. *"Yes, we will. Our little girl is going to one of the best schools in Delhi. I still can't believe it!"*

Chirag smiled, placing his hand over hers. *"Believe it. This is just the beginning of her bright future."*

They turned to Aastha, who sat on the floor, immersed in her toys, blissfully unaware of the life-changing milestone she had just achieved. Aashvi and Chirag exchanged a knowing glance, their hearts swelling with pride and anticipation—this was just the beginning of their daughter's incredible journey.

The morning sun bathed the room in a soft golden glow, as birds chirped outside, signaling the start of a new day filled with possibilities. Aashvi crossed her arms and narrowed her eyes at Chirag as he adjusted his tie, getting ready to leave for work. *"Chirag, you are just as stingy as ever! Our daughter has passed the entrance exam for one of the best schools in Delhi, and instead of celebrating, you're rushing off to the office?"* she huffed, her voice laced with playful frustration.

Chirag sighed, glancing at his watch. *"Aashvi, I have an important meeting today. My clients are flying in from overseas—I can't skip this."*

Aashvi rolled her eyes dramatically. *"Dinner happens at night, Mr. Workaholic! I'm not asking you to miss your meeting. I'm just saying, take us out to celebrate in the evening. We deserve it!"*

Chirag smirked, knowing there was no winning against her when she set her mind to something. *"Fine, we'll go for dinner tonight. You find a good place, and I'll take care of the rest."*

Aashvi's face lit up with excitement. *"What's there to search? We're going to Jama Masjid! We'll have some amazing kebabs and biryani—real food, not your fancy restaurant stuff."*

Chirag chuckled, shaking his head. *"You and your love for street food! Alright, Jama Masjid it is. But only if you promise to let me eat in peace without making me take a hundred pictures for Instagram."*

Aashvi laughed, stepping closer and straightening his tie. *"Deal. But only if you promise not to talk about work during dinner."*

Chirag smiled, pressing a quick kiss to her forehead. *"Deal."*

As he walked out the door, Aashvi called out after him, *"And don't be late! Aastha and I will be ready before you even step into the house."*

He waved over his shoulder, already looking forward to the evening—a rare break from their daily routine, a chance to celebrate their little girl's achievement, and, more than anything, a moment of joy with the two people who meant the world to him.

The bustling lanes of Jama Masjid welcomed Aashvi, Chirag, and their little daughter with open arms, wrapping them in a fragrant embrace of sizzling kebabs, slow-cooked nihari, and warm, pillowy sheermal. The night air carried the tantalizing aroma of burning charcoal, mingling with the faint sweetness of cardamom and saffron from nearby sweet shops. The streets pulsed with life—vendors calling out their specialties, the rhythmic clang of steel plates, and the laughter of families gathered around tiny food stalls, savoring the rich flavors of Old Delhi.

"Jama Masjid is not just famous for its beauty, but also for its irresistible food," Aashvi murmured, glancing around at the countless eateries, each boasting a unique delicacy.

Chirag nodded, scanning the area. *"It's impossible to decide what to eat first with so many choices. But if we're here, we can't leave without tasting Qureshi's legendary seekh kebabs."*

Aashvi grinned. *"Then what are we waiting for? Let's go!"*

They found a small, traditional eatery tucked between centuries-old buildings, its rustic charm adding to the authenticity of the experience. Settling into a modest wooden table, they watched as the server arrived, placing a plate of freshly cut onions, vibrant green chutney, and lemon wedges before them.

Moments later, a sizzling plate of seekh kebabs arrived, their rich aroma instantly making Aashvi's mouth water. The skewers of minced meat glistened under the dim lights, perfectly charred on the outside yet tender within.

Chirag picked up a lemon wedge and gently squeezed it over the kebabs, the citrusy tang blending effortlessly with the smoky spices. Aashvi took her first bite, savoring the explosion of flavors—earthy, fiery, and laced with the essence of age-old Mughlai traditions.

"These kebabs…" she said, pausing to close her eyes in delight, *"it's as if the chefs have magic in their hands. The spices, the texture—no place can match this."*

Chirag smiled, watching her enjoy the meal. *"That's the magic of Jama Masjid. It's not just food—it's an experience."*

Chirag placed a crisp note on the steel tray, nodding at the waiter with a satisfied smile. "Your kebabs were exceptional," he praised. The waiter, a man who had likely spent decades serving food lovers in these lanes, gave a grateful nod before moving on to the next eager customer.

Turning to Aashvi, Chirag ran a hand through his hair and asked, *"Alright, what's next? What does madam desire now?"*

Aashvi smiled mischievously. *"Now, we treat our little princess to something sweet. Aastha loves desserts, and what better than Mohabbat ka Sharbat and Shahi Tukda?"*

With their daughter nestled between them, they strolled through the lively, aroma-filled streets of Jama Masjid, stopping at a small stall where a vendor was expertly ladling out glasses of the famed Mohabbat ka Sharbat. The bright pink drink, infused with cold milk, fresh watermelon chunks, and a hint of rose essence, looked as inviting as ever.

Chirag handed a glass to Aastha, who took a small sip before breaking into an adorable grin. *"Mmm! So sweet, Papa!"* she chirped, her tiny hands gripping the cold glass.

Aashvi chuckled. *"Of course, my love. This is called Mohabbat ka Sharbat. Love always tastes sweet."*

Chirag took a sip and sighed in satisfaction. The chilled, fragrant drink was refreshing, perfectly balancing sweetness with the coolness of watermelon. It was an experience, a sip of Old Delhi's timeless romance.

Just beside the sharbat stall, a large iron griddle sizzled with golden-brown slices of Shahi Tukda—crispy, deep-fried bread soaked in thick, saffron-infused rabri, garnished with slivers of almonds and pistachios. The vendor expertly plated a portion and handed it over.

As Chirag took his first bite, his eyes lit up. *"This… this is divine,"* he murmured.

Aashvi smirked, playfully nudging him. *"Told you so."*

Aastha, her mouth smeared with creamy rabri, giggled in delight, making both her parents laugh.

As they finished their desserts, Chirag stretched his arms and said, *"Now, I think it's time for something legendary. Aslam Butter Chicken?"*

Aashvi's eyes sparkled with excitement. *"Yes! I've heard so much about it, but I've never had the chance to try it."*

"Then let's not waste a moment," Chirag said, taking Aastha's little hand in his own. *"Tonight, we feast like true food lovers."*

Hand in hand, the trio made their way through the narrow streets once more, their hearts full, their taste buds tingling in anticipation, and their souls basking in the magic of Old Delhi's unforgettable flavors.

As they stepped inside, the small yet vibrant eatery was packed with people, all drawn by the promise of Aslam's famous butter chicken. The dim yellow lights cast a cozy glow over the rustic interiors, while the rhythmic clatter of plates and the sizzle of the tandoor created a melody of flavors.

Aashvi took a deep breath, her eyes lighting up. *"This place smells divine! I can already taste the richness in the air."*

Chirag grinned. *"Wait till you take the first bite. No one—I repeat, no one—makes butter chicken like Aslam!"*

Aastha, tugging at her father's sleeve, whined impatiently. *"Papa, I'm starving! Order fast!"*

Chirag laughed and signaled the waiter. *"Bhaiya, ek half butter chicken, rumali rotis and chicken lollipop."*

The waiter nodded with a knowing smile and disappeared into the kitchen. Within moments, their table was graced with the star dish—a steaming plate of creamy butter chicken, drenched in golden, velvety butter sauce, with a hint of smoky tandoori aroma. Freshly baked rumali rotis, glistening with melted butter, sat beside it, waiting to be torn apart.

Aashvi picked up a piece of chicken, letting the sauce drip as she took the first bite. Her eyes widened as the flavors burst in her mouth. *"Oh my God, Chirag! This is... incredible. The cream, the butter, the spices—it's perfect!"*

Chirag smirked, dipping his roti into the sauce. *"Told you! Aslam's magic is unbeatable."*

Aastha, not wanting to be left behind, took a small piece, carefully dipping it in the butter-laden gravy before taking a bite. Her eyes sparkled as she clapped her hands. *"Yummy! Mumma, papa, I want to eat this every day!"*

Chirag chuckled. *"Looks like we have a new butter chicken fan in the family!"*

As they ate, enjoying every bite, the world outside seemed to fade away. The richness of the butter melted on their tongues, the hint of spice tingled their senses, and the laughter they shared made the meal even more special.

As their plates emptied, Aashvi leaned back, completely satisfied. *"I don't think I can ever eat butter chicken anywhere else again. This place has ruined me!"*

Chirag wiped his hands with a napkin and smiled. *"That's what good food does—it leaves a mark not just on your taste buds but on your memories."*

Aastha, still licking the butter off her fingers, grinned. *"Mumma, papa, today was the best day ever!"*

With their hearts full and their cravings satisfied, they stepped out into the bustling streets of Old Delhi, carrying the taste of Aslam Chicken not just in their mouths, but in their memories—a night of food, laughter, and togetherness they would cherish forever.

The morning sun cast a golden hue over the quiet street as Chirag and Aashvi stood by the roadside, waiting for the yellow school bus to arrive. Chirag held Aastha's school bag, a bright Mickey Mouse-shaped backpack, in one hand, and a water bottle in the other. Aashvi, holding Aastha's tiny fingers in her own, crouched beside her, gently brushing a stray strand of hair from her daughter's face.

"Beta, today is your first day of school," Aashvi said softly, her voice filled with a mixture of excitement and concern. *"Be good, listen to your teacher, pay attention in class, and take care of yourself, okay?"*

Aastha, dressed in her crisp new school uniform, nodded enthusiastically, but the slight nervousness in her big, curious eyes didn't go unnoticed.

Just then, the school bus pulled up, its bright yellow paint gleaming under the morning sun. The cheerful chatter of children inside echoed as the doors swung open. Chirag bent down and gently lifted Aastha onto the bus steps, handing her over to the bus helper, who took her bag and water bottle.

For a brief moment, Aastha turned around, her tiny hands gripping the edge of the bus seat as she looked at her parents with wide eyes. Chirag and Aashvi forced a smile, waving at her with encouragement, though their hearts felt heavy. It was the first time their little girl was stepping into the world on her own.

As the bus started to move, Aashvi clutched Chirag's arm, her eyes slightly misty. *"She's growing up so fast, isn't she?"* she whispered.

Chirag let out a deep breath, watching the bus disappear down the street. *"Yes, she is… and today marks the beginning of her new journey."*

Meanwhile, inside the bus, Aastha slid into a seat, looking around at the unfamiliar faces, her fingers gripping the strap of her uniform tightly. But then, she took a deep breath, just as her mother had taught her, and gave herself a tiny nod.

A new chapter of her life had begun.

The school bus came to a smooth halt outside the grand school entrance. As the doors swung open, the bus helper began assisting the children, one by one, as they stepped down. Being a new admission, Aastha hesitated for a moment. The helper gently took her tiny hand, guiding her inside while carrying her water bottle and backpack over his shoulder.

As they entered the school premises, a mesmerizing sight greeted her. A lush green garden, filled with vibrant, blooming flowers, stretched across the courtyard. The fragrance of fresh blossoms lingered in the air, and the soft chirping of birds echoed gently. In the background, the school building stood tall and majestic, its glass windows glistening under the golden rays of the sun.

The helper led Aastha through the long corridors, filled with soft murmurs and hurried footsteps, before finally settling her on a vacant seat inside a brightly lit classroom. With a reassuring nod, he walked away, leaving her alone among unfamiliar faces. Aastha sat still, her small fingers clutching the edge of her dress, her eyes filled with curiosity and nervousness as she observed the children around her.

Suddenly, the sharp ring of the school bell filled the air, startling her. In an instant, the classroom buzzed with movement as children rushed excitedly towards the playground. Aastha, confused and unsure of what to do, remained seated, looking around helplessly.

Just then, a young boy with bright eyes and a warm smile approached her.

"Hello! What's your name?" he asked cheerfully.

Aastha hesitated, her voice barely above a whisper. *"My name is Aastha."*

The boy chuckled. "Why are you sitting here? It's prayer time! Come on, let's go to the ground!"

Before she could think twice, he gently took her hand, and together, they walked towards the school assembly area, where rows of students stood neatly, ready for the morning prayer. As the hymn began, Aastha took a deep breath and joined in, her nervousness slowly melting away into the rhythm of her new journey.

The morning sun cast a golden glow over the vast school ground, where hundreds of students stood in perfectly aligned rows, dressed in crisp uniforms. The air buzzed with a mix of excitement and discipline as the teachers took their places near the stage. The school building, towering in the background, reflected the warm sunlight, while the fluttering national flag added a sense of pride to the atmosphere.

Aastha, standing amidst her new classmates, nervously clasped her hands together. She had never been part of such a grand assembly before. The boy who had guided her to the ground gave her an encouraging smile.

A loud clang of the bell signaled the beginning. The head boy, standing at the front, spoke into the microphone, his voice firm and clear.

"Attention, everyone! Stand straight for the morning prayer."

A hush fell over the ground. The students, in perfect synchronization, closed their eyes and brought their hands together in a gesture of prayer. A melodious tune filled the air as they began to sing the morning hymn.

"We shall overcome
We shall overcome
We shall overcome, someday

Oh, deep in my heart
I know that I do believe
We shall overcome, someday

We shall be alright
We shall be alright
We shall be alright, someday..."

The words echoed through the open space, blending harmoniously with the chirping of birds. Aastha hesitated at first, unsure of the lyrics, but soon, she found herself mouthing the words, feeling a strange sense of belonging.

As the prayer ended, the principal took the stage, his presence commanding respect. *"Good morning, students,"* he greeted, his deep voice carrying across the assembly.

"Good morning, sir," the students responded in unison.

Aastha was mesmerized. Everything felt so new, yet strangely comforting.

Next came the thought of the day, followed by the news report, where a student read out the latest national and international headlines. Then, the sports captain announced upcoming events, and the assembly concluded with the national anthem.

As the final words of *"Jana Gana Mana"* filled the air, Aastha stood tall, a newfound excitement rising within her. This was just the beginning—her journey at school had truly begun.

Back in class, Aastha sat quietly at her desk. Just as she was settling in, the door creaked open, and the teacher walked in. A tall, kind-looking woman in a simple saree, her hair neatly tied back, stepped inside.

"Good morning, children," the teacher greeted as she entered the class.

In an instant, the entire class stood up to show respect. All except one.

Aastha, unaware of the tradition, remained seated. She looked around, confused as the other students stood straight. The teacher's gentle eyes landed on her, a kind smile forming on her lips.

"We have a new face in the class today. What's your name, dear?" she asked.

Aastha hesitated for a moment before softly replying, *"My name is Aastha, ma'am."*

"Welcome, Aastha! Tell us something about yourself."

Aastha took a deep breath and stood up. *"I live in Lajpat Nagar. My father is a software engineer, and my mother is a housewife."*

The teacher smiled warmly. *"That's wonderful. You are such a sweet girl. Welcome to our school."* She then turned to the class. *"Children, today is your first day in LKG. I am your class teacher, and I will also be teaching you maths."*

The day unfolded smoothly. The teacher took introductions from every child, making sure each one felt comfortable. Then, the lessons began.

Aastha sat beside Sandeep, the boy who had helped her during the assembly. During lunch, she hesitated at first, but then Sandeep smiled and offered her a piece of his sandwich. She giggled and shared her food in return.

By the end of the day, they were laughing like old friends.

The final school bell rang, signaling the end of the day. Aastha climbed onto the bus, her tiny hands clutching her water bottle tightly. As the bus rolled through the streets, her heart swelled with excitement and relief.

As soon as the bus stopped near her house, she spotted her mother, Aashvi, standing by the gate, eagerly waiting.

"Beta! How was your first day?" Aashvi asked as she hugged her little girl.

Aastha sighed. *"Mumma, at first, I was scared. I didn't know what to do. But then... Sandeep helped me!"*

Aashvi raised an eyebrow. *"Sandeep? Who's Sandeep?"*

Aastha's face lit up. *"He's my classmate! He showed me where to go during the assembly, and we sat together in class. Mumma, we even shared lunch!"*

Aashvi smiled, brushing Aastha's hair back. *"Oh! So you already made a friend on your first day?"*

Aastha nodded enthusiastically.

Hand in hand, they walked toward their home, Aastha chattering excitedly about her new friend, her new school, and the many adventures yet to come.

Chirag walked through the gate of his home, exhausted from a long day at work. His tie was slightly loosened, and his bag hung lazily from his shoulder. But the moment he stepped inside, a familiar, excited voice filled the air.

"Paaapaaaa!"

Before Chirag could even register, a tiny whirlwind came rushing toward him—Aastha, his little angel. Her small feet barely touched the ground as she ran, her pigtails bouncing with every step.

She leaped forward, trying to wrap her tiny arms around his waist. Chirag, caught off guard but filled with warmth, dropped his bag to the floor and lifted her effortlessly into his arms.

He hugged her tightly, feeling the soft rhythm of her heartbeat against his chest. Kissing her forehead, he whispered, *"Meri gudiya ka pehla din kaisa raha?"*

Aastha pulled back slightly, her eyes sparkling with excitement. *"Papa, pehle to mujhe bohot darr lag raha tha... main akeli thi, kuch samajh nahi aa raha tha..."* she pouted, recalling the morning.

Chirag's brows furrowed with concern. *"Phir kya hua?"* he asked gently.

Aastha's expression changed instantly. Her pout turned into a wide grin. *"Phir Sandeep aaya! Papa, usne mujhe assembly le gya, class me mere sath baitha, aur humne lunch bhi share kiya!"*

Chirag raised an eyebrow playfully. *"Oh! Toh pehle hi din ek dost bhi ban gaya?"*

Aastha nodded eagerly, her little hands clutching onto his shirt. *"Haan papa! Sandeep bohot accha hain. Usne mujhe har jagah guide kiya!"*

Aashvi, who had been standing at the door, watching the heartwarming moment, smiled as she walked closer. *"Maine kaha tha na, school jaane ke baad sab theek lagne lagega?"* she said, caressing Aastha's head.

Aastha beamed up at her mother and then looked back at Chirag. *"Papa, aaj school bohot maza aaya!"* she giggled.

Chirag let out a chuckle, spinning her around in the air before gently placing her back on the floor. *"Meri beti toh bohot brave nikli!"* he said proudly.

As Aastha continued to chatter about her day, describing every little detail with animated gestures, Chirag and Aashvi exchanged a knowing glance. Their daughter was growing up—learning, exploring, and finding her way in the world.

A Journey to Remember: The School Trip

The evening sun painted the sky in shades of orange and pink as Aastha rushed into the living room, her face glowing with excitement. She could barely contain herself as she looked at her mother, who was folding clothes on the sofa.

"Mummy, my school is organizing a trip to Jaipur! All my friends are going. Can I go too?" she asked eagerly, her eyes filled with hope.

Aashvi smiled, sensing her daughter's enthusiasm. *"I don't have a problem, beta, but we'll have to wait for your papa to come home. He will make the final decision. You can ask him when he gets back,"* she said, placing a neatly folded t-shirt on the pile.

Aastha pouted, crossing her arms. *"But if you ask him, he'll agree immediately!"*

Aashvi chuckled. *"I'll try, but I can't promise anything."*

The rest of Aastha's day passed in a blur. She could already picture herself exploring the beautiful hills of Jaipur with her classmates. The anticipation made her restless, and every few minutes, she would glance at the clock, waiting for her father to return.

Finally, the sound of the main door unlocking made her heart leap. Chirag had arrived home from work. He placed his laptop bag on the table and sighed, sinking into the sofa.

Aastha knew this was her moment, but instead of asking him right away, she decided to start smartly.

"Papa, should I bring you a glass of water?" she asked sweetly.

Chirag looked at her, surprised. He turned to Aashvi and raised an eyebrow. *"Is she feeling okay? Since when does she offer to get me water? She must want something from me."*

Aashvi smirked. *"Why don't you ask her yourself when she comes back?"*

A few moments later, Aastha returned, carefully carrying a glass of water. *"Here, Papa. Have some water,"* she said with an innocent smile.

Chirag took a sip, then leaned forward, narrowing his eyes. *"Alright, Aastha. What do you want?"*

"Papa, you know I always care about you," she began, trying to butter him up.

Chirag chuckled. *"Straight to the point, Aastha."*

She took a deep breath. *"Papa, my school trip is going to Jaipur, and I really, really want to go! Mummy has already promised me—now you just have to say yes."*

Chirag turned to Aashvi. *"You promised her?"*

Aashvi raised her hands in defense. *"I made no such promise! I only told her to ask you."*

Chirag looked at Aastha thoughtfully. *"Beta, you are in eighth grade. You are still too young for such trips. There won't be anyone to take care of you."*

Aastha had expected this. She had her argument ready. *"Papa, all the students are going! If every parent thought like this, schools would have to cancel all trips. Plus, our teachers will be there to take care of us. Please, Papa, I've never asked you for anything before. Just this once—please let me go!"* She looked at him with pleading eyes.

Chirag sighed, shaking his head. *"Alright, you can go. If it means this much to you, I'll talk to your class teacher and complete all the formalities."*

"Yay!" Aastha squealed in delight and hugged her father tightly.

But she wasn't done yet. *"Papa, there's one more thing,"* she said with a mischievous smile.

Chirag raised an eyebrow. *"And what is that?"*

"I need to go shopping! I need new dresses for the trip!"

Aashvi rolled her eyes. *"You already have plenty of dresses. Wear those."*

"But I've already worn them all, Mummy! I need something new. And I was talking to Papa, so you should stay out of it," Aastha teased.

Chirag smiled, shaking his head. *"Fine, beta. Tomorrow evening, go to Central Market with Mummy and buy what you need. Just don't go overboard."*

Aastha beamed. *"Thank you, Papa! You're the best!"*

As she danced around the living room in excitement, Chirag turned to Aashvi with a sigh. *"Looks like we're raising a little negotiator."*

Aashvi laughed. *"She takes after you."*

Chirag smirked. *"Then we're in trouble."*

They both chuckled as they watched their daughter twirl around, already lost in her dreams of Jaipur.

It was evening, and Aastha's impatient voice echoed through the house.

"Mummy, hurry up! We're getting late for the market. Who takes this long to get ready?" she called out.

Aashvi stepped out of her room, adjusting her dupatta. *"Have you ever noticed how much time you take to get ready?"* she asked with a teasing smile.

Aastha rolled her eyes. *"Mummy, let's not start an argument now. We can debate later—right now, we need to leave!"*

With a chuckle, Aashvi shook her head and booked an auto. Within minutes, they were on their way to Central Market, Lajpat Nagar, ready for an exciting shopping spree.

The sun was beginning to set, casting a golden glow over the bustling streets of Central Market, Lajpat Nagar. The air was filled with the aroma of street food, the chatter of eager shoppers, and the honking of rickshaws weaving through the crowded lanes.

Aastha and Aashvi stepped out of an auto, and Aastha's eyes lit up with excitement. *"Wow, Mummy! It's so crowded today! Look at all the beautiful dresses!"* she exclaimed, pointing towards a shop displaying colorful kurtis and trendy Western outfits.

Aashvi smiled, adjusting her dupatta. *"Yes, beta. Central Market is always full of life. Now, let's focus on what we need—no unnecessary shopping!"* she warned.

"But, Mummy, shopping is meant to be fun, not just a checklist!" Aastha giggled, already pulling her mother towards a boutique.

They entered a small but stylish fashion store, where mannequins were dressed in the latest Indo-Western fusion outfits. Aastha immediately picked up a light pink floral dress with delicate embroidery.

"Mummy, isn't this just perfect for my trip?" she asked, holding the dress against herself and twirling in front of the mirror.

Aashvi examined it closely. *"It's nice, but do you really need another pink dress? You already have so many!"*

"But this one is different! Look at the embroidery—so elegant!" Aastha pleaded with puppy eyes.

The shopkeeper, sensing an opportunity, smiled and said, *"Madam, yeh dress imported design ka hai, lightweight aur comfortable bhi. School trip ke liye perfect rahega!"*

Aashvi sighed, giving in. *"Alright, try it first."*

Aastha rushed to the trial room and came out, looking absolutely delighted. *"Mummy, it fits perfectly! I love it!"*

After bargaining a little, they paid for the dress and moved to the next shop, where Aastha picked up a denim jacket and a pair of trendy sneakers for casual outings during the trip.

As they walked past the bustling stalls, Aastha's eyes landed on colorful earrings and bangles displayed at a street vendor's cart.

"Mummy, I need these jhumkas!" she said dramatically, holding up a pair of oxidized silver earrings.

"You don't need them, beta. You just want them," Aashvi corrected with a knowing smile.

"Exactly! And what's the harm in wanting something pretty?" Aastha grinned.

Aashvi laughed. *"Fine, but this is the last item we're buying."*

After completing their shopping spree, they decided to take a break at a chaat stall, where Aastha happily munched on a plate of crispy golgappas while Aashvi sipped on masala chai.

"Best shopping day ever!" Aastha sighed contentedly.

Aashvi chuckled, watching her daughter's joy. *"Just wait till Papa sees the bill."*

Both mother and daughter laughed, enjoying their special shopping day before Aastha's big trip.

Chirag and Aashvi stood at the school gate with Aastha, watching the excitement unfold before them. Two large tourist buses were parked outside, their bright colors reflecting the joy of the students boarding them. Laughter and chatter filled the air as children, dressed in vibrant casual outfits, climbed into the buses, some placing their luggage carefully in the compartments while others waved excitedly at their friends.

Aastha, her eyes gleaming with anticipation, was part of the cheerful commotion. Just then, a familiar voice called out—

"Namaste, Uncle and Aunty! Hi, Aastha!"

Aashvi glanced at the boy standing beside Aastha. *"And who is this?"* she asked with curiosity.

"Mummy, this is Sandeep," Aastha introduced him with a smile.

Aashvi greeted him warmly. *"Oh, so you're Sandeep! We've heard a lot about you from Aastha. How are you, beta?"*

"I'm good, Aunty! How about you?" he responded politely.

Aashvi nodded. *"I'm doing well."*

As they engaged in lighthearted conversation, a loud honk from the bus interrupted them. The driver leaned out, signaling everyone to take their seats.

"Time to go!" Sandeep grinned, pulling his backpack over his shoulder.

Aastha eagerly climbed into the bus and quickly grabbed a window seat, with Sandeep settling beside her. She turned towards her parents one last time, her face a mix of excitement and nervousness.

Chirag leaned in and placed a reassuring hand on her shoulder. *"Take care, beta. Enjoy yourself, but be careful."*

Aastha smiled. *"Don't worry, Papa! I'll be fine—everyone's here with me."*

The engine roared to life, and as the bus slowly pulled away from the school, the students inside waved at their parents. Chirag and Aashvi waved back, their hearts swelling with both pride and longing.

As the bus disappeared down the road, Aashvi sighed. *"Our little girl is growing up so fast."*

Chirag smiled, watching the empty road ahead. *"Yes, she is. And this is just the beginning of her adventures."*

The bus moved steadily towards Jaipur, the city lights still a few hours away. The journey was long—almost 300 kilometers—but for Aastha, it felt like time was slipping away too fast. She sat by the window, mesmerized by the changing landscapes, the open fields, and the distant silhouettes of hills. The fresh air that brushed against her face carried a sense of adventure, but she had no idea that this journey would take an unexpected turn.

Beside her, Sandeep was watching her carefully, his fingers nervously playing with the edge of his seat. He had rehearsed this moment in his head a hundred times, yet he couldn't find the right words. And then, without thinking, he reached out and held Aastha's hand.

Aastha gasped and turned sharply towards him. *"What are you doing, Sandeep? Have you lost your mind?"* she whispered, her eyes wide with shock.

Sandeep took a deep breath. *"I've wanted to tell you something for a long time, Aastha… but I never got the chance. Today feels like the right moment."*

Aastha raised an eyebrow. *"What is it? Just say it clearly."*

Sandeep hesitated for a second, then spoke in a firm voice. *"I have liked you since LKG."*

Aastha blinked, unsure whether to laugh or be serious. *"LKG? Seriously? Who even understands love at that age?"* she scoffed.

Sandeep smiled softly. *"Maybe I didn't understand it back then. But I knew there was something special about you. And over time, that 'liking' turned into something deeper."*

Aastha shook her head, pulling her hand away. *"Wow, so now it's love? Just a minute ago, you were saying you 'liked' me, and now you're in love? Are you sure you haven't had something to drink?"* she teased.

Sandeep chuckled. *"Love doesn't happen in a second, Aastha. It starts with liking someone, admiring them, and then one day, you just realize—they mean everything to you."*

Aastha sighed, shifting her gaze back to the window. *"Look, first of all, let go of my hand. People are watching."*

Sandeep immediately let go, but his eyes remained on her, waiting. The bus continued its journey, the low hum of the engine blending with soft romantic songs playing in the background. The moment felt surreal—a love confession in the middle of a school trip.

After a long silence, Sandeep finally spoke again. *"You still haven't given me an answer."*

Aastha frowned. *"Answer? What answer?"*

Sandeep sighed. *"I just told you I love you. Don't you think I deserve a response?"*

Aastha rolled her eyes. *"And what exactly do you expect me to say? You love me—fine. But I don't know what to do with that information. Why are you acting like a heartbroken Devdas?"*

Sandeep smirked. *"Because love needs an answer, Aastha. I need to know what you feel."*

Aastha hesitated for a moment before replying, *"We are really good friends, Sandeep. And honestly, I've never thought of you in that way."*

Sandeep leaned back in his seat, nodding. *"Then start thinking about it now."*

Aastha exhaled in frustration. *"Oh, so now you want me to decide in a minute? Sandeep, love isn't a math problem. Some things take time. And right now, I just want to enjoy this trip without any emotional drama. So please, for now—just sit quietly and stop bothering me."*

Sandeep smiled, leaning closer. *"Fine. I'll wait. But don't take too long, okay?"*

Aastha shot him a glare but couldn't help the small smile playing on her lips. She turned back to the window, watching the trees blur past as the bus moved forward.

She had no idea what the future held—but something told her that this trip would change everything.

The clock struck 5 PM as the bus rolled to a stop in front of Hotel Rajasthan Palace, an elegant heritage-style hotel, pre-booked for the school trip. The golden glow of the setting sun cast a warm hue on the grand façade, making the entire building look surreal. Excitement buzzed in the air as students peered out of the windows, their eyes widening in awe at the beautiful architecture.

As the doors of the bus opened, the hotel staff, dressed in traditional Rajasthani attire, stood at the entrance, ready to welcome the students. Some held trays with refreshing drinks, while others carried garlands, offering a traditional welcome.

"Wow, this place looks amazing!" Aastha gasped, stepping down from the bus.

"It's like a royal palace!" another student chimed in.

Laughter and chatter filled the air as the students began to exit, stretching their stiff limbs after the long journey. Teachers gathered at the reception, discussing room allocations, while the staff efficiently unloaded the luggage.

But amidst all the excitement, Sandeep remained quiet. His usual cheerful expression had faded, replaced by something unreadable. He walked beside Aastha, but his eyes were lost somewhere else.

Aastha noticed his silence and nudged him lightly. *"Hey, what's wrong? You look like you just saw a ghost."*

Sandeep shook his head, forcing a smile. *"Nothing... just tired, I guess."*

"Liar." She narrowed her eyes. *"You were fine on the bus, and now suddenly you look like you've lost a cricket match."*

Sandeep let out a small chuckle but didn't respond. Instead, he turned his gaze towards the grand chandelier hanging inside the hotel lobby, avoiding her eyes.

Meanwhile, the teachers announced, *"Alright, students! Boys and girls will be staying on separate floors. Check your assigned rooms on the list at the reception. Once you get your keys, settle in quickly. We will gather in the banquet hall for dinner at 8 PM."*

The students eagerly rushed to check their room numbers. Aastha scanned the list and found her name.

"Room 204, second floor. What about you?" she turned to Sandeep.

He checked the list and sighed. *"Room 307, third floor."*

"Different floors, huh?" Aastha said, a little disappointed.

"Well, rules are rules." Sandeep shrugged.

Aastha gave him a playful look. *"Or maybe the universe is keeping you away from me because you were acting weird just now."*

Sandeep smirked slightly. *"Or maybe the universe wants you to miss me."*

Aastha rolled her eyes but smiled. *"Go, get some rest. Maybe you'll finally tell me what's on your mind at dinner."*

He hesitated for a second, then softly said, *"Maybe I will."*

As they walked towards their rooms, the grand corridors of Rajasthan Palace echoed with excitement, laughter, and whispers of young hearts—some eager for adventure, some battling emotions they could no longer ignore.

Aastha lay on her bed, staring at the ceiling, but her mind was far from the grand hotel room she was in. Sandeep's words echoed in her heart, stirring emotions she had never truly acknowledged before.

"Mujhe tumse pyar ho gaya hai, Aastha…"

She had always seen him as her best friend, her constant companion since childhood. But tonight, something felt different. His touch, his words, the way his eyes held a depth she had never noticed before—it all played in her mind like a melody she couldn't ignore.

Aastha lay on her bed, resting after the long journey. The soft glow of the bedside lamp cast a warm light across the cozy hotel room. The curtains were slightly drawn, allowing the cool evening breeze to drift in, carrying the faint aroma of Rajasthani spices from the banquet hall below.

Just as she was about to close her eyes for a few moments, her phone buzzed. Without thinking, she quickly picked it up, assuming it was one of her friends. But as she glanced at the screen, she saw *"Papa Calling..."* flashing across the display.

She immediately sat up and answered, *"Hello, Papa!"*

Chirag's voice came through, a mix of relief and mild irritation. *"Beta, have you reached Jaipur?"*

Aastha smiled. *"Yes, Papa! We arrived around 5 PM. The hotel is beautiful."*

Chirag sighed on the other end. *"And you didn't think to call and inform us? Your mother and I were so worried! We kept trying to reach you, but your phone wasn't connecting."*

Aastha bit her lip, realizing her mistake. *"Papa, I'm so sorry! There was a network issue; otherwise, I would have definitely called."*

There was a brief silence. Then, Chirag's tone softened. *"Alright. Are you happy there?"*

Aastha grinned. *"Very! Everything here feels so royal. And with all my friends around, it's even more fun!"*

Chirag chuckled. *"That's good to hear. Just take care of yourself and make sure you eat on time."*

Aastha glanced at the time—7:45 PM.

"Papa, I have to go for dinner by 8 PM. I'll call you later, okay?" she said, already hopping off the bed to freshen up.

Chirag sighed dramatically. *"Alright, you've grown up now. Now even your papa's words have to wait."*

Aastha giggled. *"Oh, come on, Papa! Don't say that! Love you!"*

"Love you too, beta," Chirag smiled. *"Take care."*

As the call ended, Aastha sighed happily, stretching her arms. Her first night in Jaipur had just begun, and the excitement of the trip was only getting started.

Aastha stepped into the grand banquet hall of the hotel, her eyes widening at the mesmerizing décor. The golden chandeliers cast a warm glow, illuminating the intricately carved wooden panels on the walls. The aroma of rich Rajasthani cuisine filled the air—spicy curries, fragrant rice, and freshly baked rotis being served on beautifully decorated platters.

She spotted Sandeep already seated at a table near the large glass window, which overlooked the glittering cityscape of Jaipur. He waved at her with a soft smile. Aastha hesitated for a moment, her heart fluttering slightly as she walked towards him.

"You took so long!" Sandeep teased as she sat down.

"I was talking to Papa," Aastha said, adjusting her chair. *"He was worried since I didn't call after reaching."*

Sandeep chuckled. *"Typical parents. But that's sweet. At least someone cares about you more than I do."*

Aastha rolled her eyes but couldn't hide the small smile that formed on her lips.

The servers arrived, placing steaming dishes on their table—dal baati churma, gatte ki sabzi, and a variety of pickles. The colors of the food looked as vibrant as the city itself. Aastha picked up a piece of baati, dipped it into the rich dal, and took a bite. The flavors exploded on her tongue.

"Mmm… this is amazing!" she said, savoring the taste.

Sandeep watched her with amusement. *"You look so happy when you eat good food."*

She laughed. *"Of course! Good food is happiness."*

The evening continued with laughter, conversations, and stolen glances. Every now and then, their hands would brush accidentally, sending tiny sparks through Aastha's heart. The feeling was new, unfamiliar, yet comforting.

As they finished their meal, Sandeep leaned slightly closer. *"So, are you enjoying Jaipur so far?"*

Aastha met his gaze, her eyes reflecting the golden lights around them. *"I think... this trip is going to be unforgettable."*

Sandeep smiled. *"I hope it is... for both of us."*

A warm silence settled between them as the soft melody of Rajasthani folk music played in the background. That night, amidst the royal setting of Jaipur, something beautiful was beginning to unfold—something neither of them fully understood yet, but both could feel deep within.

The night was calm, the air filled with a gentle breeze that carried the distant melodies of folk music playing somewhere in the city. Aastha and Sandeep walked side by side through the softly lit corridors of the hotel, their footsteps echoing in the quietness. Their hands brushed against each other, sending an electric sensation through their skin. And then, without a word, Sandeep gently took Aastha's hand in his.

Aastha glanced at him, her lips curling into a soft smile. She didn't pull away. There was something warm, something right about that moment. They kept walking, lost in the silent conversation of their gazes.

Just a few steps away, a group of senior boys stood at the corner, watching them closely. Among them, Aviraj's eyes darkened with jealousy as he noticed Sandeep holding Aastha's hand.

"Did you see that?" Aviraj muttered, his jaw tightening. *"They're walking hand in hand. Something is definitely going on between them."*

His friend smirked. *"I thought they were just friends."*

"There's no such thing as just friendship between a boy and a girl," another boy chimed in. *"This is love."*

Aviraj's fists clenched at those words. *"Love?" he scoffed. "No. Aastha is mine. And I won't let anyone take her away from me."*

His friend raised an eyebrow. *"So, what are you planning to do now?"*

Aviraj smirked darkly. *"Just watch. This story has only begun."*

Meanwhile, completely unaware of the envious eyes on them, Aastha and Sandeep reached her room. She hesitated for a moment before turning to him.

"Sandeep..." she whispered.

He looked at her, his eyes searching hers. *"Hmm?"*

She opened her mouth as if to say something but then smiled instead. *"Good night."*

Sandeep chuckled softly. *"Good night, Aastha."*

She stepped inside, closing the door behind her. Her heart was beating faster than usual. Something was happening between them—something delicate, something unspoken.

But neither of them knew that their budding love had already caught the attention of someone who would do anything to separate them.

The morning sun painted the sky in soft hues of gold and pink as Jaipur awoke to a new day. The air carried a slight chill, making the warmth of the sun even more comforting. Aastha stood by her hotel window, gazing outside with a soft smile. Today was special—they were going to visit Hawa Mahal, one of Jaipur's most enchanting landmarks.

By the time she was ready, Sandeep was already waiting for her near the bus. As always, they sat together, the familiar presence of each other bringing a quiet comfort. The journey was filled with laughter and chatter, but Aastha found herself lost in the excitement of exploring Jaipur's royal history.

The bus came to a halt outside Hawa Mahal, and the students stepped out, their eyes widening at the grand pink structure standing before them. The delicate lattice windows, the towering façade, and the aura of centuries-old royalty surrounded them like a timeless dream.

"Wow..." Aastha whispered, her eyes shining. *"It's even more beautiful than I imagined."*

Sandeep chuckled beside her. *"And here I thought nothing could capture your attention more than food."*

She playfully nudged him. *"History is just as fascinating... sometimes."*

Their tour guide, an elderly man with a deep, commanding voice, gathered the students.

"Welcome to Jaipur, the Pink City," he began. *"Founded in the 17th century by Maharaja Sawai Jai Singh, Jaipur is famous for its grand palaces, historical forts, beautiful gardens, and rich cultural heritage."*

As they walked closer, the guide continued, *"Today, we begin our tour with Hawa Mahal, built in 1799 by Maharaja Sawai Pratap Singh under the architectural guidance of Lal Chand Ustad. This structure, standing 80 feet tall, was designed to resemble the crown of Lord Krishna."*

Sandeep leaned in slightly and whispered to Aastha, *"A palace designed like a crown? That's kind of poetic, don't you think?"*

She nodded, mesmerized by the thought.

The guide gestured toward the intricate 365 jharokhas (small windows) of the palace. *"These windows were designed to allow cool breezes to pass through, keeping the palace pleasant even during the scorching summers. That's why it's called Hawa Mahal—the Palace of Winds."*

Aastha ran her fingers along the delicate carvings on the walls, feeling the history embedded in the stones. *"It's incredible how they built this without modern technology,"* she said, her voice filled with awe.

The guide led them to a secret passageway, revealing the hidden ramps that once allowed royal women to be carried up in palanquins without being seen by the outside world.

"This palace was not just an architectural marvel," the guide explained, *"but a symbol of tradition. The royal women were not allowed to step outside freely, so they would sit behind these latticed windows and observe the bustling streets of Jaipur without being seen."*

Aastha paused in front of one of the windows, imagining a time when queens and princesses sat here, longing for a world they could only witness from afar.

"It must have been lonely," she murmured.

Sandeep watched her closely. *"Maybe. Or maybe they found beauty in watching life unfold from behind these windows."*

Aastha turned slightly, a small smile playing on her lips. *"Just... how beautiful this place is. So much history, so many untold stories."*

Sandeep smirked. *"And yet, here you are, lost in your own story."*

She looked at him, sensing the shift in his tone. There was something different in his eyes today—something intense, something raw.

Before she could speak, he took another step closer. The space between them was almost nonexistent now. *"You know, Aastha… right now, I feel like hugging you."*

Her breath hitched. *"Sandeep!" She stared at him, her cheeks burning. "Have you lost your mind? What are you even saying?"*

He didn't flinch, didn't look away. *"I love you, Aastha. I have for a long time. And I can't pretend anymore."*

Her heart pounded against her ribs. *"Sandeep… love isn't just about saying it. There's a time, a place for everything. You can't just—"*

"Why not?" he interrupted, his voice laced with urgency. *"Why do we always wait for the 'right time'? What if this is the right time? What if I don't want to waste another moment without you knowing how much I need you?"*

Aastha looked away, struggling to find the right words. She had always known there was something between them—something unspoken, something undeniable. But was she ready to name it?

She exhaled slowly, then met his gaze. *"Sandeep… I won't lie. You are special to me. I feel something for you, but love... love is a big word. I need time to understand my own feelings."*

His eyes softened. *"And if I say I'll wait? No matter how long it takes?"*

A small smile tugged at her lips. *"Then maybe… one day, you'll get your answer."*

Sandeep studied her for a moment before stepping back, his lips curving into a knowing smile. *"I'll hold you to that, Aastha. Because some things are worth waiting for."*

"Alright, kids, our tour of Hawa Mahal is now complete. Next, we're heading to The City Palace. Everyone, please take your seats on the bus," the guide announced.

As the bus rolled through the picturesque streets of Jaipur, the students gazed out at the vibrant cityscape. Within moments, they arrived at the grand City Palace, ready to step into a world of royal history and architectural splendor.

"Alright, everyone! It's time to visit the majestic City Palace. Please step out and follow me," the guide announced.

Aastha and Sandeep walked side by side, taking in the grandeur of the entrance. The towering gates, adorned with intricate carvings, opened to reveal a magnificent courtyard leading deeper into history.

"This palace was built by Maharaja Sawai Jai Singh II in 1729," the guide continued as they walked through the entrance. *"It is a stunning blend of Rajput, Mughal, and European architectural styles. Every corner of this palace tells a story of its glorious past."*

Sandeep leaned toward Aastha and whispered, *"Imagine living here… waking up to this beauty every day."*

Aastha chuckled, *"I'd probably get lost in one of these courtyards before breakfast."* The guide led them further inside, stopping in front of a beautifully designed structure. *"This is Mubarak Mahal,"* he said, gesturing toward the elegant building with delicate arches. *"It was originally built to welcome royal guests. Now, it has been converted into a textile gallery, where the royal attires of kings and queens are displayed."*

As they stepped inside, they were greeted by a mesmerizing display of silk robes, embroidered turbans, and ornate jewelry that once belonged to the Maharajas and Maharanis. Aastha traced her fingers along the protective glass, admiring the fine craftsmanship of the fabrics. *"Can you believe how heavy these outfits must have been?"* she murmured. Sandeep smirked. *"And yet, they carried themselves with so much grace. Maybe you should try wearing one."* She rolled her eyes playfully. *"Yeah, right! I can barely walk in a simple dress."*

The group moved ahead towards another grand chamber. *"Now, we are entering Diwan-e-Khas, also known as Sarvato Bhadra Chowk,"* the guide announced. *"This was the private audience hall where the Maharaja held meetings with his ministers and soldiers. Common people were not allowed here."*

Aastha looked around in awe. The grand hall had crystal chandeliers, gold-painted walls, and two massive silver urns placed in the center.

"These silver urns," the guide pointed, *"are the largest silver vessels, made by melting 14,000 silver coins. Maharaja Madan*

Singh II was deeply religious, and he carried Ganga water in these urns when he traveled to England."

Sandeep's eyes widened. *"That's dedication!"*

Aastha smiled. *"It's fascinating how faith played such a big role in their lives."*

They walked further toward a beautifully adorned gateway. The guide stopped and gestured to the artwork. *"And here we have Ridhi Sidhi Pol—the four intricately designed doorways, each dedicated to a different season and deity."*

Aastha ran her fingers lightly over the carvings. *"Each one is so unique..."*

"Yes," the guide nodded. *"The Peacock Gate represents autumn, Lotus Gate symbolizes summer, Green Gate stands for spring, and Rose Gate represents winter."*

"Even their doors tell stories," Aastha whispered, mesmerized.

Sandeep smiled, watching her fascination. *"Some things are meant to be admired forever,"* he said softly.

She turned to him, meeting his gaze, and for a moment, the history around them faded as they stood there, caught in their own timeless moment.

The palace stood tall, whispering secrets of the past, while two hearts unknowingly began writing their own story amidst its ancient walls.

Their days in Jaipur had been nothing short of enchanting, woven together with golden sunsets, whispered histories, and stolen glances. The city had opened its arms to them, and in its embrace, something delicate yet profound had begun to bloom.

At Gaitor Ki Chhatriyan, the air had been thick with echoes of the past, the intricately carved cenotaphs standing as silent sentinels of Rajasthan's royal legacy. Aastha had traced her fingers lightly over the cool marble, feeling the weight of centuries pass through her touch. Nearby, Sandeep had watched her, a soft smile playing on his lips, as if memorizing the moment.

At the Sun Temple, they had stood together at the edge of time, watching as the dying sun bathed the city in hues of gold and crimson. The sky had stretched infinitely above them, yet the space between them had never felt smaller. *"If a sunset could last forever,"* Aastha had whispered, more to herself than to him. Sandeep had simply looked at her, as if she were the most breathtaking view of all.

The Galta Ji Temple, nestled within the folds of rugged hills, had wrapped them in an unexpected serenity. The soft murmur of sacred waters and the chatter of playful monkeys had been their only audience as they wandered through the temple complex, their footsteps falling into an unspoken rhythm. Aastha had dipped her fingers into the cool, holy water, her reflection rippling beneath the surface. Sandeep, standing beside her, had only seen one thing in that reflection—her.

In the tranquil embrace of Kanak Vrindavan Park, surrounded by emerald greens and the distant silhouette of Jal Mahal, they had found a rare, quiet moment. No words. No rush. Just the sound of the wind, the rustling leaves, and the unspoken emotions hanging between them. Jaipur's streets had seen many love stories before, but in those fleeting moments, the city had whispered that this one was different.

The bustling bazaars, the intoxicating aroma of freshly made ghewar, the rhythmic beats of Rajasthani folk music—every corner of Jaipur had held a memory, a promise. Their steps had drawn them closer, not just to the city, but to each other.

But all journeys, no matter how beautiful, must find their pause.

Back in Delhi, the city pulsed with its usual chaos—blaring horns, hurried footsteps, neon-lit streets. And yet, something had shifted. Jaipur had left its imprint, not just on their memories, but on their hearts.

The Era of Love

Aastha sat on the couch, flipping through her math textbook, frustration evident on her face. She sighed and looked up at her mother, Aashvi, who was folding clothes nearby.

"Mummy, I'm really struggling with math," Aastha admitted, closing the book. *"Until 8th grade, I managed with your and Papa's help, but now it's getting tougher. I think I need coaching."*

Aashvi looked at her daughter thoughtfully. *"We've never stopped you from studying, Aastha. If you feel you need coaching, you can start. Your Papa will be home soon—I'll talk to him about it."*

Aastha's face lit up. *"Thank you, Mummy!"*

Aashvi smiled. *"But wait—you haven't told me where you want to take coaching. Have you found a good institute?"*

Aastha nodded eagerly. *"Sandeep goes to a coaching center in South Ex. There's a teacher named Mr. Jain—he explains math really well. A lot of students from our class study there."*

Aashvi considered for a moment before replying, *"Alright. I'll discuss it with Chirag and let you know."*

That evening, Sandeep was scrolling through his phone when it suddenly rang. Aastha's name flashed on the screen. Smiling, he picked up the call.

"Hello, Aastha! How are you?"

"I'm good, Sandeep! I talked to Mummy about the coaching classes."

"Oh? What did she say? Did she agree?" Sandeep asked curiously.

"Not yet," Aastha replied. *"She said she'll talk to Papa first before making a decision."*

Sandeep chuckled. *"And what if they don't agree?"*

Aastha's voice was confident. *"They never say no when it comes to my studies. Mummy has practically agreed—she just needs Papa's opinion."*

Sandeep smiled. *"That's great! Then I guess I'll be seeing you at coaching soon."*

Aastha laughed. *"Hopefully! Let's see what Papa says."*

As they ended the call, Aastha felt a new excitement bubbling inside her. A new step in her academic journey was about to begin, and with Sandeep by her side, she knew it would be an experience to remember.

Love is a feeling, gentle and true,
A silent whisper, yet speaks to you.

Love is a blessing, a gift from above,
A cure for pain, a song of love.

Love is a hope, a reason to live,
A flame in the dark, with light to give.

Love is the sunrise, warm and bright,
Love is the moon, in the softest light.

The golden afternoon sun bathed the school ground in a warm glow as Sandeep and Aastha sat on the grass, sharing their lunch. Their bond had deepened over time, and now, there was no hesitation in their closeness.

Sandeep took a bite of his sandwich before turning to her. *"Aastha, you still haven't accepted my love,"* he said, his voice laced with longing.

Aastha smiled softly. *"Love isn't something you just accept with words, Sandeep. It's something you feel."*

Sandeep leaned in slightly, his gaze searching hers. *"I know you love me too. But sometimes, you have to tell your partner how much they mean to you."*

Aastha looked into his eyes, her heart beating a little faster. Then, in a voice just above a whisper, she said, *"Fine. If words are what you need, then listen carefully—I love you, Sandeep. More than you can ever imagine."*

Just as the moment settled between them like a warm embrace, an unwelcome presence disrupted their peace.

Aviraj and his group of friends walked up and casually took a seat beside them. His presence sent a chill through the air.

"I love you too, Aastha," Aviraj said, his voice carrying an unsettling arrogance. *"But you never gave me a chance. You've ignored me for too long."*

Sandeep's fists clenched. His jaw tightened as he stared at Aviraj. *"How dare you speak to her like that?"* he said, his voice low and dangerous.

Aviraj smirked, unfazed. *"You think she belongs to you?"* He laughed coldly. *"You should stop dreaming, Sandeep."*

Before Sandeep could react, Aviraj suddenly raised his hand and slapped him across the face. The sharp sound echoed in the silence of the schoolyard.

Aastha's breath hitched. A storm of anger surged within her, and without a second thought, she stood up and struck Aviraj hard across his cheek.

"How dare you lay a hand on Sandeep!" she seethed, her voice unwavering. Her eyes burned with fury.

Aviraj stared at her, stunned, as the sting of her slap registered.

"And listen to me carefully," she continued, her voice cutting through the tension like a blade. *"I will never be yours. Do you hear me? I have always been Sandeep's, and I always will be. We love each other, and no one—especially not you—can change that."*

Aviraj's smirk vanished. His friends shifted uncomfortably, realizing the tables had turned.

"If you ever try to come between us again, I won't hesitate to report you," Aastha added, her tone sharp and final.

For the first time, Aviraj had nothing to say. He stood there for a moment, then turned on his heels and walked away, his friends following in silence.

Aastha turned to Sandeep, concerned, flickering in her eyes. *"Are you okay?"* she asked, her voice softer now.

Sandeep, still holding his cheek, smiled despite the pain. *"I think I just fell in love with you even more."*

She rolled her eyes, but her lips curled into a smile. *"Good. Because I meant every word I said."*

And with that, the world around them faded, leaving only the unshaken strength of their love.

Aviraj stormed away, his fists clenched, his breaths ragged with anger. Never in his wildest dreams had he imagined that a girl—especially the one he loved—would slap him in front of the entire school. His pride, his ego—shattered in an instant.

The school ground still buzzed with murmurs, but for Aviraj, time had come to a standstill. His face burned, not just from the sting of the slap but from humiliation. His eyes, red with rage, fixed on Aastha. She stood beside Sandeep, her posture strong, her expression unwavering. There was no regret in her gaze, no fear—only defiance.

Something twisted inside him.

"You humiliated me in front of everyone, Aastha..." he muttered under his breath, his jaw tightening. *"You'll pay for this."*

His friends stood around him, shifting uncomfortably. One of them hesitated before saying, *"Forget her, man. She never liked you anyway."*

But Aviraj wasn't listening. His eyes remained locked on Aastha, as if burning a hole through her. His rage wasn't just anger anymore—it was something darker, something more dangerous.

"I won't let this go so easily," he whispered, a sinister determination creeping into his voice. *"If she can't be mine... I'll make sure she doesn't live in peace either."*

His friends exchanged uneasy glances. They had seen Aviraj angry before, but this was different. This was personal.

Aviraj took a deep breath, his hands trembling with the force of his emotions. The love he once felt had been swallowed by something else—obsession, vengeance.

And obsession had a way of turning even the purest of feelings into something monstrous.

Love, when one-sided, has a way of turning into something dark—something destructive. And Aviraj was no exception. His obsession had consumed him, blinding him to reason, drowning every ounce of logic he once had. The humiliation he suffered in front of the entire school had ignited a fire inside him—one that burned with vengeance.

Sitting on a dimly lit street corner with his colony friends, Aviraj lit a cigarette, taking a deep drag before exhaling slowly. His jaw was clenched, his knuckles white as he gripped the lighter. His friends sat around him, listening intently as he spoke, his voice laced with quiet fury.

"She slapped me. In front of the whole damn school," he muttered, his eyes dark with resentment.

One of the guys smirked, shaking his head. *"And you just let her go? Damn, man, you lost your respect today."*

Aviraj's grip on the cigarette tightened. He turned to the guy, his lips curling into a cold smile. *"I let her go? No... I was just waiting for the right moment."*

He flicked the cigarette onto the ground, crushing it under his shoe. His voice dropped to a chilling whisper. *"Now, I'll make sure she regrets ever crossing me. I'll ruin her reputation. I'll tear her pride apart, just like she tore mine."*

Another friend leaned in, intrigued. *"So, what's the plan? You need help, just say the word."*

Aviraj's eyes gleamed with something dangerous. He had made up his mind. This wasn't just about love anymore—it was about power, about proving that no one could humiliate him and walk away unscathed.

"She thinks she won today," he murmured, a sinister smirk playing on his lips. *"But the game has only just begun."*

Aviraj sat alone on the rooftop of his house, staring at the city lights that stretched endlessly before him. The cool night breeze brushed against his face, but it did nothing to calm the storm raging inside him. His fists clenched as memories of Aastha flashed before his eyes—her laughter, the way she used to tuck her hair behind her ear, the way she had looked at Sandeep, not him.

He had spent years loving her, convincing himself that she was meant to be his. And yet, she had chosen someone else. The thought burned inside him like a flame refusing to die.

Just then, his best friend Rohan climbed up the stairs and sat beside him. He didn't speak at first, simply looking at Aviraj with knowing eyes. Then, after a moment, he said, *"You know, love isn't about winning someone. It's about valuing them."*

Aviraj scoffed. *"Easy for you to say. You don't know what it feels like to watch the person you love walk away with someone else."*

Rohan sighed, shaking his head. *"No, I don't. But I do know this—if you truly love someone, you don't destroy them just because they don't love you back. You respect their feelings, their choices."*

Aviraj looked away, his jaw tightening.

"Think about it, Aviraj," Rohan continued gently. *"If you really love Aastha, wouldn't you want her to be happy? Even if that happiness isn't with you?"*

Aviraj swallowed hard, his chest tightening at the words. He had been so consumed by his own desires, his own pain, that he had never stopped to think about hers. Had he ever truly loved her, or had he just wanted to own her?

"Love isn't about possession," Rohan's voice softened. *"It's about respect. And if you ever truly loved her, then let her go... with dignity, not with hate."*

A long silence stretched between them. The weight of Rohan's words settled deep within Aviraj's heart, shifting something inside him. He took a deep breath, looking up at the stars above.

Maybe love wasn't about fighting for someone. Maybe, sometimes, love meant stepping back... and letting go.

Love is not just about having someone,
It's a feeling, pure like the morning sun.
If you love them, cherish their choice,
Respect their feelings, hear their voice.

If their heart belongs to someone new,
Let them go with a smile, let love stay true.
For love is freedom, not a chain,
Not a reason to cause them pain.

Not every love is meant to last,
Some are just lessons from the past.
If they leave, let them be,
Love is about setting them free.

If love is real, there's no demand,
No force, no grip, just an open hand.

For love with respect is love indeed,
Without it, it's just a selfish need.

If your love brings only pain,
Then it's just a stubborn game.
True love is where joy survives,
Not where only one heart cries.

The hum of the city wrapped around them as Aastha sat behind Sandeep on his bike, the cool evening breeze playing with her hair. The streetlights flickered as they weaved through the bustling roads, leaving behind the quiet lanes near their coaching center. It had been two months since her coaching classes had begun, and with her father's approval, she had settled into a routine—sometimes traveling with Sandeep, other times taking public transport. But evenings like these, when they stole a little extra time for themselves, felt special.

"Aastha, I'm craving something good tonight," Sandeep mused as they rode along.

"Me too," she admitted with a smile. *"But where should we go?"*

Sandeep thought for a moment before shrugging. *"No idea."*

"We've never been to Moolchand, right?" Aastha suggested. *"I've heard people come from far just to have the parathas there."*

"I've heard about it too," Sandeep nodded. *"But I never really got a chance to go."*

"Well, tonight's our chance," she grinned.

As they sped through the streets, Aastha's hands lightly rested on Sandeep's shoulders, and without realizing it, she leaned forward, her head resting against him. The warmth of his presence, the steady rhythm of his breathing—it felt safe, familiar. She closed her eyes for a moment, just feeling the ride, the evening, and the quiet connection between them.

They reached Moolchand and parked the bike in a small roadside space, the air instantly filled with the rich, mouthwatering aroma of sizzling butter and freshly made parathas. The narrow lanes were alive with the sounds of people chatting, vendors shouting orders, and the occasional hiss of a tawa meeting molten ghee.

"Here we are—Moolchand's famous paratha shop," Sandeep announced as they approached.

Aastha scanned the menu, her eyes lighting up. *"I want gobhi paratha!"* she declared.

Sandeep chuckled. *"I'll go with aloo."*

"You get the order; I'll find us a table," Aastha said, glancing around at the crowded space.

Since it was a self-service stall, Sandeep went to place the order while Aastha managed to grab a small wooden bench tucked in a corner. The evening felt alive here—smiling faces, groups of friends sharing laughter over plates of crispy parathas, couples stealing quiet moments amid the chaos.

A few minutes later, Sandeep returned with two steaming hot parathas placed on metal plates. The golden-brown bread glistened with butter, and beside them sat fresh onion rings, fiery green chilies, and a bowl of tangy chutney.

"*Smells heavenly,*" Aastha sighed as she tore a piece of her gobhi paratha.

Sandeep took a bite of his aloo paratha and nodded approvingly. "*Totally worth the hype.*"

For a while, they didn't speak much—just exchanged glances, shared little smiles, and savored the warmth of their food. In that simple, unplanned moment, under the open sky and amidst the aroma of spices, there was no rush, no worries—just them, two souls, and a plate of parathas.

As Aastha reached for another bite, she glanced at Sandeep. "*Let's do this more often,*" she murmured.

Sandeep smirked. "*Are you talking about the parathas or…?*"

She rolled her eyes but laughed. "*Maybe both.*"

And in that laughter, under the neon glow of a streetlamp, a quiet promise lingered—of more nights like this, of stolen moments, of something that didn't need words to be real.

An Unforgettable Night

Sandeep's fingers tightened around his phone as he paced outside the coaching center, his heart pounding at an obnoxious pace. The streetlights flickered above him, casting long shadows on the pavement as if amplifying his dread. With a deep breath, he dialed Aastha's home number.

Aashvi picked up almost immediately. *"Hello, Sandeep? Is everything okay?"*

His voice was laced with worry. *"Aunty, Aastha didn't come to coaching today, and her phone has been switched off for hours. Do you know where she is?"*

Aashvi's heart skipped a beat. *"What? But she left home at 4 PM for coaching. Are you sure she wasn't there?"*

Sandeep swallowed hard, his chest tightening. *"I waited for her, asked around. She never came."*

A nervous silence filled the air. Aashvi's heart pounded as she immediately dialed Chirag's number, her fingers trembling slightly.

"Chirag, Aastha left for coaching, but no one knows where she is. Her phone is off."

Aashvi's voice wavered, fear creeping into her tone. *"Sandeep just called me. He's there. She never showed up. And now, it's past 7 PM."*

Silence. A deafening, suffocating silence.

Then, Chirag stood up abruptly, his mind racing. *"Three hours… and no sign of her?"*

Aashvi felt her throat tighten. *"This isn't like her. She always keeps her phone on… even if it's low on battery, she finds a way to inform us."*

Chirag exhaled sharply, running a hand through his hair. *"Damn it. Something is wrong."*

A lump formed in Aashvi's throat. The walls of their home suddenly felt suffocating, closing in with every passing second.

"What if she's in trouble?"

Chirag's eyes darkened. His voice was low but firm. *"I don't care what it takes. I'm going to find her."*

And just like that, the night that had once been ordinary turned into a nightmare.

Aashvi paced back and forth in the living room, her hands trembling as she clutched her phone. Her voice casted a trembling spell with a hammering heart.

"It's been so long, and there's still no sign of Aastha!" she cried, looking at Chirag with tear-filled eyes. *"Her phone is still switched off. We've called all of her friends, but no one knows anything!"*

Chirag took a deep breath, trying to stay calm. *"Maybe we should ask a few more people before going to the police. Let's not panic just yet."*

Aashvi turned to him, her voice rising in desperation. *"Not panic? Chirag, it's been hours! She left for the coaching at 4 PM, and it's already late. We don't know where she is, we don't know if she's safe!"*

Chirag placed a hand on her shoulder, trying to reassure her. *"I understand, but we need to think logically. Let's check with her coaching center, maybe someone saw her there."*

Aashvi shook her head, tears rolling down her cheeks. *"And what if they didn't? What if something has happened to her? We have to go to the police now, Chirag! Every second we wait could be dangerous!"*

A heavy silence filled the room as the weight of her words settled in. Chirag exhaled slowly, his resolve breaking. He nodded.

"Alright. Let's go to the police."

The air inside the police station felt heavy, more like suffocating. Aashvi sat on the worn-out wooden bench, her hands clutching the end of her dupatta, twisting it unconsciously. Her eyes were red and swollen from crying, her breathing uneven. Chirag sat beside her, with an expressionless face, but his fingers tapping anxiously against his knee betrayed his inner numbness.

Sandeep stood near the desk, his jaw clenched, hands curled into fists. He had never felt so powerless before. The thought of Aastha—somewhere out there, alone, unreachable—sent chills down his spine.

Inspector Shama looked at them, his pen tapping against his desk. *"So, your daughter left for coaching at 4 PM and hasn't returned home?"*

Aashvi wiped her tears, nodding quickly. *"Yes, sir. It's been hours. Her phone is switched off. We've called everyone—her friends, her teachers—but no one knows anything. Please... you have to find her."*

The inspector exhaled, rubbing his forehead. *"Where does she take coaching?"*

"South Ex," Chirag answered. *"She's been going there for two months now. She usually returns by 6:30 PM at the latest."*

"And today, no one saw her?" the inspector asked, his voice firm.

Aashvi shook her head desperately. *"No, sir... nothing. It's like she just vanished."* Her voice cracked, and fresh tears slipped down her cheeks.

The inspector leaned forward. *"Any recent fights? Was anyone troubling her?"*

Sandeep hesitated. He could feel his pulse hammering in his throat. Then he spoke. *"There is... someone. Aviraj. He used to like her. But she never responded to him. He was aggressive sometimes, but she never took it seriously."*

The inspector's gaze sharpened. *"Aviraj. Do you know where he lives?"*

Sandeep shook his head. *"No... but he studies in our school. We can find out."*

Aashvi grabbed Chirag's hand, her voice barely above a whisper. *"Sir, please... Please find my daughter. I don't know if she's safe. I don't know if she's... alive."*

The words hung in the air, suffocating, terrifying.

Inspector Sharma stood up, grabbing his cap. *"We'll start looking immediately. Time is crucial. If anything happens, you'll be the first to know."*

The night dragged on, heavy and unyielding, wrapping the world in a cold, merciless silence. Aashvi's soft, muffled sobs echoed through the room, each one breaking the fragile stillness. Chirag held her tightly, his own eyes shimmering with unshed tears, the weight of helplessness pressing down on them both.

Nearby, Sandeep stood motionless, his gaze fixed on the looming door of the police station. His heart pounded fiercely, a silent prayer trembling on his lips — a desperate hope that somewhere, beyond these walls, Aastha was safe.

But time was slipping away. Somewhere out there, their little girl was waiting. And they had to find her. Before the night swallowed her completely.

On one side, Aastha found herself in an unfamiliar world—a world so terrifying that never even imagined in her darkest nightmares. It was a place beyond the reach of reason, where fear lurked in every shadow, and reality blurred into something sinister. Every breath she took carried an unfamiliar weight, every sound around her whispered a chilling warning. This was not just a place—this was a prison of the unknown, a nightmare she was forced to live.

On the other, her family remained oblivious to the horrors she faced. Unaware of the storm that had swallowed their daughter, they held onto hope, their prayers filling the air like unspoken pleas to the universe. Aashvi sat by the window, her hands trembling as she clutched Aastha's childhood photograph, tears streaming down her face.

"She must be fine," she whispered to herself, as if saying it out loud would make it true.

Chirag paced the room, his mind a battlefield of worry and determination. *"She will come back. We will find her,"* he reassured, though a crack in his voice betrayed the fear he tried to hide.

Time was slipping away, and with each passing second, the distance between Aastha and home grew wider. She was trapped in a cruel fate, lost in an unknown world — while those who loved her held onto hope, blind to the nightmare unfolding beyond their reach.

Mom, save me—hear my desperate plea,
I long to live, to break these chains, to be free.
Dad, your little princess is drowning in pain,
Writhing in agony, as each moment fades in vain.

Where are you? Come swiftly, pull me from this night,
You once swore my eyes would never weep in fright.
Yet today, these demons circle, ruthless and wild,
Threatening to shatter your helpless child.

Save me, Dad—I cannot bear this despair,
Trapped in torment, gasping for air.
If you don't come, if no one fights,
I fear I may vanish into the endless night.

Aastha lay curled in the cold, suffocating darkness, her breath hitching with every sob. The echoes of her own cries felt distant, swallowed by the vast emptiness surrounding her. Her body ached, not just from pain, but from the unbearable weight of fear pressing down on her chest. She had always believed her father's words—that he would protect her from every sorrow, that no harm would ever reach his little princess. But now, in this cruel, merciless moment, those promises felt like distant dreams.

She wanted to scream louder, to call out for her mother, for her father, for anyone who could rip her away from this nightmare. But the walls were deaf, and the shadows that loomed over her held no mercy. Every passing second felt like an eternity, and with each moment that slipped by, the hope inside her flickered, struggling to stay alive. Would they find her? Would she survive this abyss of horror? Or would she become just another lost voice, swallowed by the night?

In a cold, forsaken room shrouded in darkness, Aastha's screams tore through the silence, swallowed by the void around her. Malevolent hands inflicted unbearable torment upon her fragile body, each touch searing deeper than just flesh—reaching into the very depths of her soul. She trembled violently, not only from pain but from the overwhelming terror that consumed her, trapping her in a nightmare from which there was no escape.

She was trapped in a relentless nightmare, caught in a futile struggle against the merciless grip of fate. No matter how desperately she fought, the cruel reality refused to change. Every attempt to break free crumbled into hopelessness, leaving her trembling violently—her body wracked with agony, her soul drowning in despair.

"Someone tore at his clothes with merciless hands, while another struck him with relentless cruelty, each blow carving agony into his trembling body."

The room reeked of dampness, sweat, and something far more sinister—despair. Aastha lay on the cold, unforgiving floor, stripped of every shred of dignity. Her trembling body was bare, bruised, and bound, her wrists tied so tightly with rough rope that the skin beneath had begun to tear. The only sound that filled the suffocating darkness was her broken sobs, her voice hoarse from screaming.

"Papa... please save me..." she whimpered, but only the cruel laughter of monsters answered her.

A voice cut through the stale air. *"Bhai, I'm done. Now it's your turn. Satisfy yourself. I swear, it's the best feeling. We'll play with her body every day now."*

Laughter echoed around her, twisted and merciless. Rough hands slithered over her skin, touching, groping, as if she were nothing more than a lifeless object for their amusement. Aastha thrashed, but the ropes burned against her wrists, digging deeper with every desperate movement.

Blood pooled beneath her, its metallic scent mixing with the filth of the room. But they showed no pity. No remorse. Only hunger.

Aastha's cries filled the air again, but her voice was swallowed by their cruel taunts. No one was coming. No one would save her. And in that moment, as darkness threatened to consume her, she realized—this was no nightmare. This was her reality.

The scene was so gut-wrenching that even the heavens above would have wept. If God's eyes could ever show sorrow, this was the moment. The cruelty Aastha endured was beyond comprehension, and even the angels, who bore witness to her torment, would have cried in despair. Her pain echoed through the silence, a raw testament to her suffering. Yet, in the midst of it all, Aastha's family remained unaware, blind to the hell she was living. They were wrapped up in their own lives, oblivious to the agony their daughter was enduring, her suffering met with nothing but indifference.

But on earth, there was no one. No one to hear. No one to save her. Aastha's cries fell into the void, unanswered, as the world continued on, indifferent to the tragedy unfolding in its very midst.

The first light of dawn crept through the windows, casting a pale glow on the world outside. The sun rose with its gentle rays, as if it, too, felt the heaviness in the air, a reflection of the torment of the night before. The night had been long, full of anguish and sleepless worry, but for the family of Aashvi and Chirag, the worst had yet to come. The pain of uncertainty weighed heavily on their hearts, though they had no idea of the torment their daughter was enduring.

Aashvi and Chirag had stayed awake through the night, their minds racing with worry. Every tick of the clock seemed to drag on endlessly, and with each passing hour, their hope diminished. Their daughter, the one they had raised with love and care, was nowhere to be found. They had called everyone, searched every corner, but there was no trace of her.

Chirag's voice broke through the silence, his tone heavy with a growing sense of helplessness. *"Aashvi, we need to go to the police station. We have to find out where our daughter is."*

Aashvi, her eyes swollen from hours of crying, nodded silently. *"It's been too long. We need to do something... anything... to find her."*

They both knew that time was slipping away, and with each minute that passed, the fear that gripped their hearts only grew. They had to find their daughter. They couldn't afford to wait any longer.

With a shared resolve, they left the house, stepping into a world that seemed completely indifferent to the storm of emotions raging within them. The streets outside were bustling, life moving on as if nothing had happened, as if everything was normal. But for Aashvi and Chirag, the world had stopped. Every second without knowing where their daughter was felt like an eternity.

As they approached the police station, the weight of the situation settled in. What if it was too late? What if they couldn't find her? But there was no turning back now. They had to know. They had to search for their daughter, no matter where it took them.

The police station was enveloped in an eerie silence, as if time itself had come to a standstill. The soft glow of the lights on the walls cast deep shadows of tension and worry across Aashvi and Chirag's faces. They had stayed awake all night, consumed by the fear and anxiety over their daughter, Aastha. Fatigue was evident in their eyes, but so was the gnawing dread in their hearts. The ticking of the clock echoed through the silence, synchronizing with the rapid beats of their own hearts. Every eye was fixed on the door, waiting for it to swing open, hoping it would bring some semblance of hope.

Aashvi had taken a deep breath, her voice trembling. *"Chirag, it's been so long. Nothing has happened... We still don't know anything about our daughter. We've been waiting the entire night, but still, there's no news."*

Letting out a weary sigh, Chirag had responded, *"I understand, Aashvi. But we have to be patient. The police said they are searching everywhere. How long this will take, we don't know."*

Tears had welled up in Aashvi's eyes as fear gripped her heart. *"But time keeps slipping away, Chirag. What do we do now? What if... what if something has happened to our daughter? What will we find?"*

Placing a reassuring hand on her back, Chirag had tried to steady her. *"I know, Aashvi. But we have to trust the police. They're doing everything they can."*

Aashvi had barely held back her tears, her voice breaking. *"Do you really think so? Will she be okay? What if... what if something's happened to her?"*

Then, the heavy silence of the police station had been interrupted by the creak of the door. A police officer had stepped inside, his face weary but serious. Both Chirag and Aashvi had turned to him with a mixture of hope and dread, their hearts racing.

The officer had spoken in a calm but exhausted tone. *"We have checked with all the hospitals and conducted thorough investigations across every possible lead. We've done everything we could, but there is no new information yet."*

Aashvi's voice had been laced with both desperation and disbelief. *"What does that mean? The police have done everything, and still, there's nothing? Where could our daughter be? Who do we turn to for help now?"*

With concern etched on his forehead, the officer had explained, *"We've checked every possible location—hospitals, schools, her friends' homes. But so far, there's no news. It may take a little more time."*

Chirag had felt his frustration mounting. *"Do we still have to wait? Our daughter is nowhere to be found—should we give up hope?"*

The officer had met his gaze firmly. *"We've searched everywhere, and I want you to know, we are continuing the search. You need to give us a little more time. We're doing everything we can to find her."*

Aashvi's voice had cracked as she asked, *"Is there still a chance? Will we find her again?"*

With a solemn nod, the officer had assured them, *"We're certain we will find her. Please, just a little more time."*

As the officer had left, a fresh wave of despair had settled over them. They had sat in silence, feeling time slow down, their hearts heavy with fear.

Chirag had gently placed his hand over Aashvi's. "Aashvi, we will find her, no matter what. We have to believe that."

Through tear-filled eyes, Aashvi had given a faint smile. *"I know, Chirag. We have to find her."*

And so, they had sat quietly, trapped in a silence that carried both fear and a flicker of hope. The police station had remained eerily still, but deep within them, a fragile hope had endured—the hope that one day, their daughter would return to them.

Chirag and Aashvi had spent the entire day walking through the streets of Delhi, clutching a photo of their daughter, desperately asking everyone about her. Their hearts were heavy with worry, the pain of not knowing where she was tearing at them. But somewhere, in the dimly lit corner of a room, their daughter, Aastha, was trembling in agony, her body racked with pain, and she was in desperate need of medical care—care that was nowhere to be found.

The air in the room was thick with a chilling silence before it was broken by a cruel voice. *"Eat,"* the voice commanded, cold and unfeeling.

Aastha tried to scream, but the pain in her body was too much, shaking her to the core. She could feel her body trembling uncontrollably, her throat constricted by the agony, but still, she tried to cry out for help.

"You can scream all you want," the voice mocked, *"but no one will hear you here."*

Her hair was roughly yanked back, her head tilted to look up at the man standing over her. The pain was unbearable. She wanted to break free, to run, but there was nowhere to go.

"Stop your screaming and eat," the voice commanded again, this time with a cruel edge. *"We want to satisfy our hunger, too. You need to obey."*

Aastha could barely move, her body fighting against her every instinct, but she mustered every ounce of strength left. When the hand reached out to feed her, she did the only thing she could—she bit down hard on the hand that dared to touch her.

The man recoiled in rage, his voice low and menacing. *"That bite will cost you dearly, Aastha,"* he hissed. *"You'll soon learn the consequences of defying us. And when you do, we'll have our fun—one by one, we'll play with your body until there's nothing left."*

Aastha's pain echoed through every corner of her being, and her parents, Chirag and Aashvi, were consumed by worry. The entire city seemed like an endless maze, and every passing moment deepened their anxiety.

Meanwhile, Sandeep, just as tormented, paced back and forth outside the school. His heart raced, and his mind was clouded with frustration. The moment he saw Aviraj, he couldn't hold back any longer.

"You're the reason Aastha is missing!" he shouted, pointing an accusing finger at Aviraj. *"You've made her run away, haven't you? Because of you, she's gone, and she's distanced herself from me!"*

Aviraj, visibly shaken by the outburst, stepped back, his voice calm but firm. *"I didn't do anything!"* he responded, trying to steady himself. *"I would never think of kidnapping anyone, especially Aastha. I love her—why would I do something like that?"*

But Sandeep wasn't listening. His anger flared as he grabbed Aviraj by the collar, pulling him closer. *"Tell me where she is!"* he demanded, his voice dripping with venom. *"You know something. If you do, just tell me!"*

Aviraj, struggling to free himself from Sandeep's grip, looked him in the eye. *"If I knew where she was, I'd tell you! But I don't!"* His voice cracked with the weight of helplessness. *"I swear to you, I don't know where she is, and I'm just as lost as you are. Please, calm down."*

The second night slipped away in a desperate search for Aastha, yet she remained nowhere to be found. The city lights flickered, streets emptied, and the air grew colder, but there was still no trace of her. With every passing hour, hope thinned like mist at dawn.

Her family, her friends, and the police searched tirelessly, but all they found was silence—an unbearable silence that echoed louder than any scream. Memories of Aastha flooded their minds, each one a painful reminder of what they had lost. Her laughter, her voice, her presence—it all felt like a distant dream now, slipping further away with every second.

Morning arrived, but for Aastha's family, the night never truly ended. Darkness clung to their hearts, heavy and unrelenting. The sun rose, but its warmth never reached them. The world outside moved on, indifferent to their suffering, while they remained trapped in the agony of not knowing.

The police did everything they could. They searched every street, knocked on every door, followed every lead—but each path led to nothing. Every call ended in disappointment, every effort met with an aching void. It felt as if Aastha had vanished into thin air, leaving behind only grief in her wake.

Chirag recounted the moment his phone rang, the name flashing on the screen sending a chill down his spine—Inspector Sharma. His hands trembled as he answered the call.

He remembered saying, *"Hello?"* with a shaky voice.

Inspector Sharma's tone was firm yet calm. *"Mr. Chirag, I need some information from you."*

His heart pounded. *"Yes, Inspector. Did you find anything? Is there any news about Aastha?"* he had asked desperately.

The inspector's response had only deepened his anxiety. *"We're still searching, but I wanted to ask—what was the name of the boy who used to trouble Aastha?"*

Chirag had frowned at the unexpected question. *"Why? What happened? Did you find something?"*

But Inspector Sharma remained vague. *"Nothing yet. We just need to question him. It's part of the investigation."*

Taking a deep breath, Chirag answered, *"His name is Aviraj."*

A brief silence followed before the inspector replied, *"Alright, thank you for the information. We'll look into it."*

But Chirag couldn't hold back. *"Inspector… is there still no trace of Aastha?"* he had asked, his voice laced with desperation.

A pause. Then, Sharma had said, *"We're doing everything we can. We will find her soon, I promise."*

The call had ended, but the weight in Chirag's chest had only grown heavier. The uncertainty, the fear—it was unbearable. His daughter was still out there, lost, and every passing second felt like an eternity.

A dimly lit room, with a single chair and a table in the center. Above the table, a lone bulb swayed slightly, casting eerie shadows on the walls. The silence was thick, almost suffocating.

Aviraj sat on the chair, gripping the armrests tightly. Sweat trickled down his forehead, his throat dry, and his heart pounding against his ribs.

Then, the door creaked open. Heavy boots echoed against the floor as Inspector Sharma entered. Aviraj stiffened, his eyes darting toward the officer, fear evident in them.

Inspector Sharma pulled a chair in front of him and sat down. *"Listen, Aviraj, let's not waste time. We are under a lot of pressure. Aastha is still missing, and we need answers. So just tell us the truth—where have you hidden her?"*

Aviraj shook his head desperately. *"I don't know anything! Why would I kidnap her? What would I even gain from it?"*

The inspector leaned forward, his voice sharp. *"You kidnapped her because you couldn't handle rejection. You were madly in love with her, but she insulted you—she slapped you in front of everyone. That humiliation, that anger—it made you do this, didn't it?"*

Gritting his teeth, Aviraj shot back, *"Yes, I was angry! She embarrassed me, but that doesn't mean I would kidnap her! I would never hurt Aastha!"*

The inspector's patience snapped. In one swift motion, he struck Aviraj across the face. The sharp slap echoed through the empty room.

"Enough of these stories," Sharma said coldly. *"Just tell me the truth."*

Aviraj's eyes watered, his voice trembling. *"How can I tell you something I don't know?"*

Hours passed. The interrogation turned brutal. The officers used every method they could, but no matter how much they pressured him, Aviraj's answer remained the same—he didn't know where Aastha was.

Days slipped away silently, each one heavier than the last, and still, Aastha remained nowhere to be found. The police began to lose their grip on hope, their faces growing more weary with every passing hour. And with every tick of the clock, the gnawing fear of what might have befallen her deepened, casting a shadow over everyone who waited.

Nine long, agonizing days had stretched into an unbearable silence. Despite tireless searches, endless inquiries, and following every possible lead, the result was always the same—an echoing void where Aastha's presence should have been. Her family clung desperately to hope, but that fragile light flickered and dimmed under the weight of growing dread and despair.

In the hollow silence of those days, time seemed to stand still — as if the world itself was holding its breath, waiting for a miracle that refused to come.

Then, in the dense forests of Faridabad, something eerie began to stir. A crowd gathered, murmurs of confusion and anxiety rippling through the air. An overwhelming sense of dread filled the atmosphere, as if something terrible was about to unfold.

In the center of the gathering, there she was—a girl, lying on the ground in a state far worse than anything anyone could have imagined. She was naked, her skin pale, smeared with blood and dirt. Her body was limp, broken—almost lifeless. Her face was bruised, her eyes wide open but empty, staring into nothingness as if searching for something she couldn't find. Her tangled hair clung to her face, and her body trembled violently.

The sight was enough to freeze anyone in place. Some of the bystanders, horrified by the sight, rushed to call the police. Someone quickly draped a cloth over her frail form, trying to shield her from the stares of the onlookers.

Then, the sound of an ambulance siren cut through the tension like a blade. Its wail echoed through the quiet forest, growing louder and louder, piercing the air with a sense of urgency and dread. The police arrived with the ambulance, their faces grim.

The girl, still unconscious, was placed on a stretcher, her broken body showing no sign of movement. Her hands hung limply, her eyes unseeing, as if she had already crossed into a place beyond this world. Her body shivered uncontrollably, a faint, chilling sign that she was still clinging to life, but for how long?

As the ambulance doors slammed shut, the vehicle sped off, its sirens wailing into the distance, leaving behind a trail of fear and unanswered questions. The crowd stood still, their hearts heavy, unable to speak, only left to wonder about the horror they had just witnessed.

The forest fell eerily silent. Time seemed to stand still. No one knew who the girl was, nor could they comprehend the horror that had unfolded. But one thing was certain—the terror was far from over.

The question lingered in the air like an unspoken promise: *Who had done this, and why?*

The hospital corridors were filled with the frantic rush of doctors and nurses, all desperately trying to save a life hanging by a thread. A frail girl, her body barely clinging on to life, lay motionless on a stretcher, her shallow breaths nearly imperceptible. Medical teams hurried behind her, doing everything they could to stabilize her, their faces etched with urgency.

The police were handling the formalities, their expressions filled with worry and tension. Time was slipping away, and there was no certainty whether they could save her in time.

Chirag's phone rang, its sound slicing through the heavy silence. His hand trembled as he answered the call.

Chirag's voice trembled as he answered the call. *"Hello?"*

"Mr. Chirag, this is Inspector Sharma. We've found a girl. She's in the hospital. Can you come here? I'll send you the address," the inspector said urgently.

Chirag's heart pounded with both hope and fear. *"What do you mean? Is it her? Is it Aastha?"*

There was a brief pause before Inspector Sharma spoke again, his voice strained. *"We can't be sure yet, but we believe it might be her. She's in critical condition. Please hurry."*

Chirag's voice cracked as panic rose in his chest. *"I'm coming. Is she... is she still alive, Inspector? Please tell me she's still—"*

"Just get here, Mr. Chirag," Sharma interrupted, trying to stay calm. *"We're doing everything we can, but time is running out."*

The call ended, and Chirag stood frozen, his heart heavy with fear and a growing dread that he might be too late. He looked over at Aashvi, her face pale with anxiety, having overheard the conversation.

Her voice shook as she whispered, *"Chirag... is it really her? Please, tell me it's her. I can't take this anymore."*

Chirag's voice broke with emotion, desperate to cling to any hope. *"I don't know, Aashvi... I don't know. But we have to go now. We have to believe it's her. Please... please stay strong."*

As they rushed to the hospital, every second felt like an eternity. Their hearts pounded erratically, filled with a raw mix of hope and dread. They had no idea what they would find when they arrived, but all they could do was pray—pray that their daughter would still be there, that she would still be alive, and that their nightmare would finally come to an end.

Aashvi and Chirag stood before Inspector Sharma, their breaths heavy with fear. Chirag's hands were cold, his heart pounding against his chest. He had to stay strong—for Aashvi, for their daughter—but his voice wavered as he spoke.

"Inspector... How is Aastha? Where is she?" Chirag's voice trembled, his eyes pleading for reassurance.

Inspector Sharma let out a deep sigh. *"She is undergoing treatment... but there's something I need to show you."*

He pulled out his phone and turned the screen toward them. A bruised, fragile face stared back at them—barely recognizable, yet undeniably hers.

Aashvi gasped, her hands shaking uncontrollably. The phone slipped from her grasp and crashed onto the floor.

"No!! No!!! This can't be my Aastha! My daughter... my child... Who did this to her? Who was it? Tell me, Inspector! I won't let them live!" she screamed, tears streaming down her face.

Her cries echoed through the corridor, raw and agonizing. She collapsed to the ground, sobbing uncontrollably. Chirag, his own body trembling, bent down and picked up the phone. His heart clenched as he stared at the image—his little girl, broken, helpless. His vision blurred with tears, but he forced himself to stay composed.

He had to be strong. He had to hold Aashvi together when she was falling apart.

"Aashvi... we found our daughter... The doctors are treating her... She will be fine... We have to stay strong... for her,"

Chirag said, pulling Aashvi close, his voice choked with emotion.

Aashvi clung to him, her sobs still shaking her body.

"Inspector... my daughter... How is she now? Can we see her?" she whispered, barely able to speak.

"She is still under treatment. You can't see her right now... but the hospital's best team is taking care of her. She will recover soon," Inspector Sharma replied softly.

"Just once... let me see her... just once, Inspector," Chirag pleaded desperately.

"Not right now, Mr. Mehra Please, both of you, wait outside her room," Sharma said, his voice firm yet gentle.

A nurse approached them and, with quiet sympathy, led them toward Aastha's room. The small window on the door was covered, blocking their view, but the rhythmic beeping of machines and the hushed voices of doctors inside reminded them—she was fighting. Fighting for her life.

Chirag and Aashvi sat outside, their hands clenched together, drowning in helplessness. No words were spoken, only silent prayers and endless tears. The nightmare wasn't over. Not yet.

The hospital corridor was eerily silent, except for the rhythmic beeping of machines and the hurried footsteps of nurses rushing in and out. The smell of antiseptic filled the air, but for Chirag and Aashvi, the only thing they could sense was fear—paralyzing, suffocating fear.

Through the small glass window of the ICU, Aashvi caught a glimpse of her daughter. Aastha lay motionless on the hospital bed, her fragile body connected to countless tubes and wires. Her little chest rose and fell with each struggling breath, aided by machines that were now keeping her alive.

Aashvi's fingers trembled as she pressed them against the glass. *"She looks so weak, Chirag,"* her voice barely above a whisper. *"My baby… why isn't she waking up?"*

Chirag couldn't speak. His throat felt like it was closing up, his heart aching in a way he had never known before. He wanted to comfort Aashvi, to tell her everything would be fine—but how could he, when he himself wasn't sure?

Just then, the doctor stepped out of the room, his face grim.

"Mr. and Mrs. Mehra," he began, his tone hesitant. *"Aastha is fighting, but… her condition is critical. We are doing everything we can, but the next few hours are crucial."*

Aashvi clutched Chirag's arm, shaking her head desperately. *"No, doctor. Please, you have to save her. She's just a child… she has her whole life ahead of her."* Her voice broke, and tears streamed down her face.

The doctor sighed. *"I understand, Mrs. Mehra. But right now, all we can do is wait."*

Wait.

That was the worst part—the helplessness, the inability to do anything but watch their daughter struggle between life and death.

Aashvi's legs gave out beneath her, and she collapsed onto the chair outside the ICU. *"I should be in there with her," she sobbed. "She must be so scared… She needs me, Chirag."*

Chirag knelt beside her, his own tears slipping down his cheeks. He took her shaking hands in his. *"She's strong, Aashvi. She'll fight. She has to."* His voice cracked, betraying his own despair.

Inside the ICU, Aastha's small fingers twitched ever so slightly, as if she could hear her parents. A single tear escaped her closed eyes, sliding down her pale cheek.

She was still fighting. But for how long… no one knew.

Aastha was fighting for her life, completely unaware that she was now closer to her family than ever before. Those monsters had left her in this condition, shattering her innocence in a way beyond her conscious conception of a corrupted human. She was reduced to the lowest form of torment, one can never think of or imagine even for a split second. Such agony was lived by her.

In this world, there is only one bond that stands above all others—the bond between parents and their child. Every other relationship pales in comparison, fragile and fleeting. Couples often whisper promises of eternal love, swearing they cannot live without each other, yet a single mistake can shatter everything. Sometimes, no mistake is even needed—excuses are simply sought to break ties.

Marriages happen, vows are exchanged, but when one person leaves this world, it doesn't take long for the other to make the same promises to someone else and begin a new life. New bonds are formed, new children are born, and the cycle continues.

But when a parent loses a child, they do not search for another to fill the void. No matter how much time passes, no matter if that child was their only one—the loss remains irreplaceable, the grief eternal.

Sandeep grabbed his phone, his fingers trembling as he checked the hospital's location once again. He had to go, he had to see Aastha. Just as he reached for the door, his mother's stern voice stopped him.

"Where are you going, Sandeep?"

He turned, his heartbeat quickened.

"Aastha has been found, Maa. I'm going to see her at the hospital."

His mother's brows furrowed as she stepped forward, her voice firm.

"There is no need for you to go there."

Frustration flared within Sandeep, his hands curled into fists.

"Why not, Maa? She is my very close friend. Can't I even go see her?"

His mother inhaled sharply, concerned about shadowing her face.

"It's a police case, Sandeep. We don't know what has happened to her. You don't need to get involved in such matters."

Sandeep's chest tightened, his voice trembled with desperation.

"Maa… I love her!"

The words hung in the air, and the room fell silent. His mother's expression darkened. Before he could react, a sharp slap landed across his face.

"Stop this nonsense! This is all just an illusion. You should focus on your studies instead of getting entangled with some girl!"

Sandeep staggered slightly, his cheek burned, but the pain inside his heart was far worse. He blinked rapidly, his vision blurred.

"But Maa..."

"I have said what I had to! You will not meet her. This is my final decision!"

She turned away, her decision final. Sandeep stood frozen, every muscle in his body screamed at him to run to Aastha. But his feet refused to move. Slowly, defeated, he dropped onto the sofa, his hands clenched into his lap. His eyes remained fixed on the door, his only way out, now locked in his mother's decision.

Aastha was fighting for her life, unaware that her love had already slipped away from her. It was true what they said—during times of crisis, only family truly matters.

As Aashvi and Chirag sat beside Aastha's bed, a nurse entered the room.

The nurse said, *"Excuse me, Mrs. Aashvi, Mr. Chirag, the doctor has called for you. Please follow me."*

They stood, their hearts pounding, and followed the nurse down the hospital corridors. They reached the doctor's office, where Inspector Sharma was already waiting for them.

The doctor said, *"Please, have a seat. There is something important we need to discuss."*

Chirag asked, *"What is it, doctor? What happened?"*

The doctor answered, *"Aastha's condition has improved; she's in a better state now, and that's good news. But there's something you still don't know... about what happened to her."*

Aashvi's voice trembled as she asked, *"What do you mean? What happened to her?"*

The doctor paused, his voice heavy as he said, *"She was... raped. Not once, but multiple times. Her body has suffered severe injuries. Every part of her is badly wounded, especially her private areas."*

Aashvi gasped, her hands shaking uncontrollably. She turned to Chirag, as though searching for some comfort, but the truth was too painful to bear.

Chirag's voice was filled with anger and desperation as he asked, *"Who did this to her? Inspector, have you found anything?"*

Inspector Sharma sighed deeply and said, *"We're doing everything we can, but it's been difficult. We're still trying."*

Aashvi bitterly said, *"You've been trying for over ten days, but there's no progress. What are you actually doing, Inspector?"*

The room fell into a heavy silence, filled with frustration and helplessness. Aashvi's voice cracked as the weight of reality hit her.

Aashvi said, *"Now that we've found Aastha, they'll be caught, right? I just want her to wake up, to tell us who did this to her."*

Chirag, holding Aashvi's hand, tightened his grip, his eyes burning with a mix of pain and fury. They had waited too long for answers.

Inspector Sharma said, *"We will catch them, but right now, we need Aastha to regain consciousness. Until then, there's little we can do."*

Aashvi nodded, though her heart ached with helplessness. She knew her daughter had suffered, but she was willing to do anything to ensure that those responsible would pay for what they'd done.

Aashvi whispered to herself, *"I'll wait... for Aastha to wake up... and tell us everything."*

The hospital room was enveloped in an eerie stillness, only the soft, rhythmic beeping of the machines cutting through the heavy silence. Outside the window, the night sky stretched endlessly, the moonlight casting a pale glow over the room, adding to the somber atmosphere. Aastha lay motionless on the bed, her face bruised and swollen, her fragile body barely visible under the layers of blankets. Her injuries, evident even in the dim light, told a harrowing tale of pain and suffering.

Aashvi and Chirag sat by her side, their faces etched with exhaustion, their hands tightly clutching hers. The darkness outside mirrored the heaviness in their hearts, the quiet of the night a cruel reminder of how helpless they felt. They sat in a suspended moment—caught between fragile hope and paralyzing fear.

Aashvi's tear-streaked face was pale under the faint light, her eyes never leaving Aastha's fragile form, as if willing her to wake. Chirag sat motionless beside her, his brow furrowed in silent anguish, his heart pounding against his chest. The sterile smell of antiseptic lingered in the air, blending with the stillness, making the silence even more unbearable.

Suddenly, Aastha's fingers twitched ever so slightly.

Aashvi gasped, her heart racing. She turned to Chirag with wide, tear-filled eyes.

"Chirag... she moved!" Her voice trembled with anticipation.

Chirag leaned closer, his gaze fixed on Aastha's face. Moments later, her eyelids fluttered, struggling against the weight of unconsciousness.

"Aastha... beta!" Aashvi whispered, her voice cracking with emotion.

Slowly, painfully, Aastha's eyes opened. The light in the room was blinding, everything blurred. She winced, a soft whimper escaping her lips.

"Maa...?" Her voice was barely above a whisper, fragile like a broken melody.

"Yes, my love! I'm here, right here!" Aashvi sobbed, clutching her daughter's hand tightly as if she could anchor her back to safety.

Chirag's eyes welled up as he gently brushed Aastha's hair from her forehead. *"You're safe now, beta. The doctors are taking care of you. You just need to be strong."*

Aastha's gaze met her mother's, and in that moment, the terror she had buried deep inside resurfaced. Her body trembled as a lone tear slipped down her cheek.

"Maa... they hurt me... so much..." Her voice broke as the weight of her trauma pressed down on her.

Aashvi pulled her into a protective embrace, rocking her gently. *"No one will ever hurt you again, my child! You're safe now! We're here!"*

Aastha's tears fell freely, her lips trembling. Her fragile body shook with fear.

"Maa... I'm scared... What if they come back?"

Chirag tightened his grip on her hand. *"No, beta! No one will ever come near you again! We won't let them! The police will catch them, and they'll pay for what they did!"*

Just then, the doctor entered the room. He checked Aastha's vitals, his expression turning softer.

"This is a very good sign. She's conscious, but she needs rest. She's been through a lot," he said gently.

Aashvi wiped Aastha's tears and kissed her forehead. *"You don't have to worry about anything, my love. Just rest now... we're not going anywhere."*

Aastha's eyes, still glistening with tears, searched her mother's face. This time, they held something other than fear—relief. Slowly, exhaustion took over, and her eyes closed again.

The room fell silent once more, but now, there was a flicker of hope in that silence—a promise that she was not alone.

The soft morning light filtered through the hospital window, but it failed to bring warmth to the cold, sterile room. The steady beeping of medical equipment echoed in the silence, a haunting reminder of the thin line between life and death. Aastha lay motionless on the hospital bed, her body weak, her face marred by wounds that were not just etched on her skin but carved deep into her soul. Her trembling fingers clutched the thin hospital sheet, as if trying to anchor herself, to keep from falling into the abyss of her memories.

Inspector Sharma stepped into the room, his footsteps slow, hesitant—afraid that even the faintest sound might shatter the fragile courage Aastha was holding onto.

Aashvi and Chirag sat beside her, their eyes heavy with helpless sorrow.

"How are you feeling, Aastha?" Inspector Sharma's voice was gentle, yet firm, carrying both empathy and determination.

Aastha let out a hollow, bitter smile. "How am I supposed to feel, Inspector? I'm still alive, isn't that enough?" Her voice wavered, every word weighed down by unbearable pain.

Inspector Sharma took a deep breath and pulled a chair closer to her bed. *"We need your help, Aastha. We have to make sure those monsters face justice. Do you remember them? Do you know who they were?"*

A flicker of fear and anger flashed in Aastha's eyes. *"Not all of them… but some… they had been troubling me for a long time."*

Chirag's fists clenched at her words. *"Who were they, Aastha? Tell us!"*

Inspector Sharma leaned forward slightly. *"Were you talking about Aviraj?"*

Aastha lowered her gaze, her hands tightening around the sheet. *"No, Inspector Uncle… he used to harass me, yes… but he wasn't capable of something this monstrous. He wasn't that evil."*

"Then who? Who were the ones troubling you?" Sharma asked softly.

Aastha swallowed hard, her throat dry. *"When I used to go to my coaching class, some boys would stop me, tease me, taunt me. One of them even proposed to me once, and when I refused, they started making crude remarks every day. I was scared... but I never thought they would turn into such beasts."*

Inspector Sharma frowned. *"Why didn't you tell your family, Aastha? They could have protected you."*

Tears welled up in Aastha's eyes. Her voice was barely above a whisper, as if she was speaking more to herself than to them. *"I didn't know... I never imagined they could sink so low. I didn't want to burden my parents... I never knew... they would steal my entire life from me..."* Her voice broke, and she lowered her head, clutching the sheet tightly.

Inspector Sharma hesitated before speaking again. *"Aastha, can you tell us what happened that night?"*

Aastha's entire body stiffened. Her breathing grew ragged, and she seemed to shrink into herself. *"No... don't make me remember... I can't... I can't..."*

Aashvi took her hand, gripping it gently yet firmly. *"You are safe now, Aastha. No one can hurt you anymore. But we need to know... please."*

Aastha inhaled shakily, but the moment she closed her eyes, the walls around her crumbled, and the past came crashing down on her, drowning her in its unbearable weight.

"I left home that evening to go to my coaching class... but I never made it there. A car pulled up behind me. Before I could even turn around, a cloth was pressed over my mouth. I struggled... but whatever was on that cloth drained my strength. I wanted to scream, but my voice... my voice never came out. And then... darkness."

A cold shiver ran down her spine as she wrapped her arms around herself, trying to hold together the shattered pieces of her soul.

"When I woke up… I was lying on a cold floor. The room was dark… the air reeked of alcohol and sweat. My head was spinning… my body felt numb. And then I saw them… eight men… sitting around, drinking, laughing… as if I was just some toy thrown at their feet. I begged… I pleaded… but they didn't stop. They tore my clothes… they… they…"

Her voice broke, fading into silent sobs. The room felt suffocating, the weight of her words pressing down on everyone.

"I fought back… I tried to resist… but every time I did, they hit me. Pulled my hair, kicked me, used whatever they could find to hurt me. I lost count of how many times…" Aastha's hands curled into fists, her nails digging into her skin.

Inspector Sharma's face was grim, his own fists clenched tightly. *"Did you hear their names? Anything that could help us find them?"*

Aastha let out a bitter, empty laugh. *"When I was unconscious, I heard one of them say… 'She's of no use now. There's no life left in her. Let's get rid of her.' And then… someone wrapped their hands around my throat. Everything went black. I thought… I thought I was dead. But when I woke up… I was here."*

Silence filled the room, heavy and suffocating. Chirag wiped away his tears, his nails digging into his palms to keep himself from completely breaking down. Aashvi pressed her hand over her mouth, muffling her sobs.

Inspector Sharma exhaled sharply, his eyes burning with fury. *"We will find them, Aastha. And we will make sure they never see the light of day again. This is my promise to you."*

Aastha gave a weak nod, exhaustion overtaking her. *"I just… I just want to be free. Free from these memories… from this pain. I just want to sleep without their shadows haunting me. Is that too much to ask?"*

Chirag reached out, placing his hand over hers. *"You are not alone, Aastha. You never were. And you never will be."*

Aastha took a shaky breath, her fingers tightening around his hand. Maybe… just maybe… she wasn't completely broken yet.

Several days had passed, yet Aastha's screams still echoed in the hearts of her loved ones. Inspector Sharma had made a promise—to bring those monsters to justice. And today, that promise was about to be fulfilled.

The morning sun cast its soft glow over the city, but today felt different. The sharp wail of police sirens shattered the silence, spreading a wave of anticipation through the air. On the outskirts of the city, a decrepit warehouse stood, surrounded by armed officers. This was the dark hideout where the monsters had been lurking, believing they would never be caught.

"Surround the building! No one escapes!" Inspector Sharma's commanding voice rang out, his eyes burning with the fury ignited by Aastha's pain.

As the officers stormed in, chaos erupted. The culprits, lost in their drunken stupor, were jolted awake by the intrusion.

"*Hands in the air! Get down on the ground!*" a constable barked.

Panic spread across their faces. Some attempted to flee, but the police had them surrounded. One of them, Rajeev, bolted towards the back exit, only to be tackled to the ground by an officer. Vikrant, in desperation, reached for a knife, but before he could lift it, Inspector Sharma delivered a swift, crushing kick, sending him crashing against the wall.

"Did you think you'd get away?" Sharma growled, grabbing him by the collar, his voice trembling with restrained rage. *"After what you did, did you really believe the law wouldn't find you?"*

One by one, the perpetrators were thrown to the ground, their hands shackled in cold steel. The arrogant smirks that once taunted Aastha had vanished, replaced by sheer terror.

Outside, a furious crowd had gathered. The news had spread like wildfire. People screamed in rage, hurling stones and spitting at them. Women stepped forward, their eyes blazing with fury.

"Did you feel no mercy that night?" one of them shouted, her voice shaking with anguish.

The monsters stood with their heads bowed, too ashamed, too afraid to meet anyone's gaze.

Inspector Sharma turned to his officers and, in an icy tone, commanded, *"Take them away. Make sure they rot in hell."*

The police vehicles sped off, carrying the culprits toward the justice they could no longer escape.

Meanwhile, in a quiet hospital room, Aastha sat by the window, gazing outside. For weeks, sleep had eluded her. But today, for the first time, a weight lifted from her chest.

Maybe, just maybe… she could finally breathe again.

The evening sky was painted in deep shades of orange and purple, yet for Aastha, the world had lost its color. She sat motionless on the living room sofa, staring blankly at her phone screen, waiting—for a call, a message, any sign... but there was nothing.

Her mother stood near the kitchen, watching her daughter's anxious face. After a deep breath, she gently spoke, *"Aastha, Sandeep isn't going to call you."*

Aastha's heart sank. She lifted her hollow eyes to meet her mother's. *"He... he didn't even come to meet me, did he?"* Her voice trembled.

Her mother fell silent for a moment before speaking softly, *"I spoke to him. He said his mother doesn't approve of him meeting or talking to you. That's why he's not answering your calls."*

It felt as though the ground had slipped beneath her. A suffocating heaviness spread through her chest. She clutched her scarf tightly, as if it were her last lifeline.

"How could he do this to me, Mom?" Her voice cracked. Tears welled up in her eyes, but she fought to hold them back. *"We were so close... He knew everything. He knew what I was going through. And yet, he left me?"*

She took a deep breath, trying to stop the storm rising within her. *"The whole world is mocking me, Mom. Every time I step outside, people don't see my body; they see my wounds.*

To them, I'm not a victim, but a criminal. As if I were the one who assaulted those monsters, not them assaulting me."

Her voice was bitter, filled with pain. *"But Aviraaj... he never blamed me. I did everything wrong. When he wanted to be with me, I ignored him. And yet, every day, he came to see me, checked on me. And the one for whom I sacrificed everything... he left me alone at my lowest."*

A suffocated sob caught in her throat. *"I was wrong, Mom. I gave my love to the wrong person."*

Her mother pulled her close into an embrace. But even in that warmth, the coldness inside Aastha remained, unyielding and unmoving.

Astha's heart had been shattered, and her world was now engulfed in darkness. Inside her, there was a silence that no one could truly understand. Her eyes held a pain that few could feel. She had lost herself in every way, as if nothing was left. Every day, she was drowning further into a sorrow she couldn't even comprehend.

Even today, her situation remained the same—sad, alone, and broken. She stood by the large window in her room, gazing outside, where the sun was setting. The sky, too, had turned dark, much like her heart, with deep shades of black and orange. She sat on the sofa, trying to connect with something, but nothing felt right.

"Astha, are you okay?" Her mother asked softly as she came out of the kitchen, walking towards her. There was a worry in her mother's voice, one that Astha could sense clearly. Her mother's heart ached seeing her like this, unable to do anything to ease her pain. The emptiness on Astha's face was the hardest thing for any mother to

witness—seeing her child in pain and being powerless to help.

Astha lowered her eyes and then gave a small, empty smile—a smile that was neither of joy nor to hide her sorrow. *"I'm fine, Mom,"* she said, but there was no confidence in her voice like before. She knew those words were just meant to comfort both her and her mother, but deep down, she didn't believe them herself.

Her mother sat beside her and took her hand gently. *"You say you're fine, but the sorrow in your eyes speaks otherwise. Would you like to share what you're feeling with me?"*

Astha took a deep breath, then silently sat beside her mother. She wanted to say something, but the words seemed at a loss of expression. There was so much she wanted to express, yet they couldn't escape her lips. She felt trapped in her own thoughts and words.

"Mom, I don't know what to do," she said softly. *"Sometimes I think everything will be okay, but then there are times when I feel like I can never make it right."*

"What happened, darling?" her mother asked, concern evident in her voice. *"What are you feeling?"*

Astha closed her eyes, and memories started flooding her mind. Sandeep... that boy, the one she had loved. The one to whom she had given everything. When Sandeep entered her life, it felt like everything was about to change for the better. The love she felt for him was real, it was deep. But the boy she had embraced without any conditions had left her. The dream in her eyes had shattered. She spent each day lost in his memories, but those memories now only caused her pain.

"Mom, I never hid anything from him. I told him everything, even my deepest thoughts. Yet he still left me. I thought he would stay, but he left me all alone. I've never been able to forgive myself."

There was an eerie silence in her voice, as if she could no longer say anything more. She had buried all her feelings inside her, and now they were seeping out as nothing but pain and tears.

Her mother pulled her into a tight embrace, trying to comfort her in any way she could. *"Sweetheart, sometimes we have to make decisions in life that lead to difficult times. But it is temporary. You are not weak. You have strength within you, Astha. And your mother is here with you."*

"But Mom, I don't feel like the person I once was. My identity, my love, everything is broken. I don't know what to do next." Astha's eyes filled with tears, and she felt as though her heart was shattering within her.

Her mother held her even closer. *"You can't break, Astha. You have so much within you, more than you realize. I've learned a lot from you. Be who you are, just as you are. Nothing in this world is permanent. Pain and sorrow, too, will fade with time. You just have to trust yourself."*

Astha slowly lifted her head and looked at her mother. She began to feel that maybe, just maybe, she could handle everything. A new glimmer of hope sparked inside her. She realized that instead of losing herself, she needed to rediscover her strength. She could move forward, not by losing Sandeep, but by finding herself again.

Both mother and daughter stood up, and her mother took Astha's hand. *"You will be fine, darling. We're together, and we'll see you happy again. Find yourself once more, and show the world how strong you are."*

Astha nodded slowly, took a deep breath, and understood that it was time to heal her broken heart. She had to find her path again, and this time, she would make her own way.

The courtroom was thick with tension as the case of the eight criminals was being heard. Aashvi and Chirag sat at the front, their faces worn and heavy with the burden of the fight they had been carrying for months. Their eyes were bloodshot from sleepless nights, their bodies exhausted, but their resolve was unbroken. They were determined that their daughter Aastha would get justice, no matter the cost.

Aashvi's hands trembled slightly, clutching the hem of her sari, but she refused to let the fear overpower her. Chirag's jaw was clenched, and his fists were tight as he stared at the eight men seated in the defendant's box. His heart was heavy with rage, but there was no room for emotion now. Only the pursuit of justice mattered.

The prosecutor called for the next witness, but the defense attorney was already speaking, trying to discredit the evidence, trying to twist the truth. Aashvi's grip tightened, and her mind raced. She remembered the countless sleepless nights, the overwhelming sorrow, and the relentless pursuit of answers. Every day felt like a battle, each one harder than the last, but they had to keep going.

"These men have taken everything from us," Aashvi whispered to Chirag, her voice trembling with a mix of sorrow and fury. *"We will not back down."*

Chirag turned to her, his eyes filled with a quiet strength. *"No matter how many threats they make, no matter how many times they try to intimidate us, we will fight. We owe it to Aastha. We owe it to ourselves."*

Despite the threats they'd received—warnings to back off, the whispers of violence that had followed them—Aashvi and Chirag remained unwavering. They had been pressured, their lives threatened, their family torn apart by the strain of it all. Some relatives had distanced themselves, unwilling to support their fight, but that hadn't stopped them. In fact, it only fueled their determination further. The more they were pushed, the harder they fought.

Aashvi's thoughts raced back to the numerous arguments with their family members, the ones who had turned their backs on them in fear. But it didn't matter. Every time they were knocked down, they stood up stronger, more resolute. They had seen the worst of humanity, but they had also seen the best—their own unshakable will, the power of love for their daughter, and the support of those who truly understood.

"We will make sure they pay for what they've done, no matter what it takes," Chirag whispered fiercely, his voice filled with a quiet, steely resolve.

As the trial carried on, Aashvi and Chirag knew their battle was far from over. But somewhere along the way, their fight had grown larger than their own grief. They were no longer standing in that courtroom just for Aastha — they were standing for every silenced voice, for every shattered childhood, for every parent who had once held their child and wondered how the world could be so cruel.

Their pain had given them purpose, and that purpose had become their strength.

This wasn't just about justice anymore — it was about change. And they had made a silent vow to themselves and to every unseen victim: *We will not stop. Not until this fight is won. Not until it means something.*

The Harsh Reality of Rape Cases in India

Rape remains the fourth most common crime against women in India. With respect to the National Crime Records Bureau (NCRB) 2021 annual report, a total of 31,677 rape cases were reported across the country, averaging 86 cases per day. This marks an increase from 2020, which saw 28,046 cases, and 2019, with 32,033 cases. Of these 31,677 cases, nearly 89% (28,147) involved perpetrators familiar with the victims. Additionally, 10% of the victims were minors, i.e., (below the legal age of consent 18 years).

India has been historically described as one of the countries with the lowest per capita rates of rape. The government also classifies consensual sex committed under the false promise of marriage as rape. Over recent years, there has been a noticeable rise in the willingness to report rape incidents, likely due to the widespread media attention given to various high-profile cases, which sparked public protests both locally and nationally. These events led to significant reforms in the country's penal code regarding rape and sexual assault.

According to NCRB's 2021 data, Rajasthan recorded the highest number of rapes among Indian states, followed by Madhya Pradesh and Uttar Pradesh. Within metropolitan cities, Delhi topped the list with 1,226 rape cases reported in 2021. Jaipur had the highest rape rate at 34 per 100,000 people. On the other hand, Kolkata reported the lowest number of rape cases among major cities, with the least rape rate.

For Aastha, that night was like a terrifying nightmare—one that could never be forgotten, no matter how hard she tried. Time moved forward, but every passing moment only pushed her deeper into the past, forcing her to relive the horror. Her wounds refused to heal. Not just the visible marks on her skin, eventually they might fade with time, but the imprints on her psyche held the custody of her soul.

Every time she closed her eyes, she was dragged back into that darkness, the echoes of her own screams haunting her mind. She yelled for help, but her voice was swallowed by the void. She begged for mercy, but it only fell on deaf ears. Now, even in safety, her body trembled at the memory of those monstrous hands, and those soul-less eyes.

Aastha was not the same girl anymore. The girl who once laughed freely, whose presence brightened the dullest of rooms, was now afraid of her own reflection.

The sound of footsteps outside her door made her flinch. A shadow moving across the room sent shivers down her spine. Even the touch of her mother—a mother who had held her with the gentlest of hands since childhood—made her recoil. Every touch, every presence felt like a threat.

She no longer trusted anyone. How could she? The people who had ruined her were once strangers, perhaps even acquaintances. The world that she once believed to be safe had betrayed her.

As days turned into weeks, the whispers grew louder. At first, people looked at her with pity. But soon, that pity was replaced with judgment.

"She must have done something wrong for this to happen."
"Who will marry her now?"
"Her life is over."

The weight of their words crushed her. Her pain was no longer just hers—it had become a scandal for others to gossip about. Relatives, friends, even neighbors began to distance themselves. No one said it outright, but their actions spoke volumes. They no longer saw her as a survivor—they saw her as a disgrace.

The man she had once loved, the one she had dreamed of a future with, was no different. He held her close in moments of joy, whispered promises of forever. But now, even his voice wavered.

"Aastha, I love you, but my family will never accept this."
"People will talk. You know how society is."
"We can't be together."

She had expected pain, but nothing could have prepared her for the moment when he turned his back on her. The person she thought would stand by her had left, proving once again that she was on her own now.

This time the tears burned in her eyes, but she refused to let them roll down. Even her tears felt like a burden now.

Her home had become her prison. Stepping outside was a battle she wasn't prepared for. Every time she walked past people, she felt their eyes on her. Were they whispering about her? Were they judging her?

Slowly, she stopped leaving her room altogether. The four walls became her world, the silence her only companion. Nightmares plagued her sleep, and during the day, the emptiness consumed her. She would stare at the mirror, searching for the girl she used to be.

"Was it my fault?"

The question tormented her. Society had already decided she was guilty, but the worst part was—she was beginning to believe it too.

While Aastha was locked away in her suffering, her parents were fighting for justice. They were determined to see her attackers punished, to make sure they paid for their crimes.

But justice was not easy to find.

Threats came their way, warning them to drop the case. Bribes were offered, pressure was applied. Even their own relatives urged them to let it go.

"Why ruin your lives over this?"
"The damage is done. Move on."

But her parents refused to back down. They had lost their daughter once—they would not lose her again to a system that protected the guilty and shamed the innocent.

Time passed, but Aastha's wounds remained as fresh as ever. Her soul still bled from the torment she had endured.

Every night, she woke up screaming. Every day, she feared the sun setting, knowing the darkness would bring back the memories.

Her body could heal. The bruises could fade. But the scars on her soul? Those would stay forever.

And society?

Society would still blame her.
Society would still stare.
Society would still whisper.

But no one—not one person—would understand that she was fighting the hardest battle of all…

The battle to keep living.

The monsters who tore apart Aastha's innocence now sit behind bars, condemned to life sentences. But no cell, no sentence, could ever match the weight of the suffering she silently carries. Justice, though served on paper, feels hollow in the face of the pain she endures each day — pain that doesn't end with a verdict.

While the world moves forward — busy, indifferent, unaware — Aastha remains caught in the long, cold shadow of her past. A place where laughter is a distant memory, and healing feels like a path too broken to walk. And though her scars are hidden, they echo louder than any scream — a quiet tragedy the world will never fully understand.

"When hardships knock at the door, most people quietly walk away. But those who stay, who stand firm through every storm — they are parents. Their support isn't out of obligation, it's born from unconditional love."